GW00370908

CURRY

CURRY

David Lee

hamlyn

Published in the UK in 1997
by Hamlyn, a division of Octopus Publishing Group Ltd
2–4 Heron Quays, London E14 4JP

This edition published 2002 by Octopus Publishing Group Ltd

ISBN 0 600 60827 1

Printed in China

NOTES

Both metric and imperial measurements have been given in all recipes. Use one set of measurements only and not a mixture of both.

Standard level spoon measurements are used in all recipes.
1 tablespoon = one 15 ml spoon
1 teaspoon = one 5 ml spoon

Eggs should be medium to large unless otherwise stated. The Department of Health advises that eggs should not be consumed raw. This book contains dishes made with raw or lightly cooked eggs. It is prudent for more vulnerable people, such as pregnant and nursing mothers, invalids, the elderly, babies and young children to avoid uncooked or lightly cooked dishes made with eggs. Once prepared, these dishes should be kept refrigerated and used promptly.

Milk should be full fat unless otherwise stated.

Meat and poultry should be cooked thoroughly. To test if poultry is cooked, pierce the flesh through the thickest part with a skewer or fork – the juices should run clear, never pink or red. Do not re-freeze poultry that has been frozen previously and thawed.
Do not re-freeze a dish that has been frozen previously.

Pepper should be freshly ground black pepper unless otherwise stated.

Fresh herbs should be used, unless otherwise stated. If unavailable, use dried herbs as an alternative but halve the quantities stated.

Measurements for canned food have been given as a standard metric equivalent.

Nuts and nut derivatives
This book includes dishes made with nuts and nut derivatives. It is advisable for customers with known allergic reactions to nuts and nut derivatives and those who may be potentially vulnerable to these allergies, such as pregnant and nursing mothers, invalids, the elderly, babies and children, to avoid dishes made with nuts and nut oils. It is also prudent to check the labels of pre-prepared ingredients for the possible inclusion of nut derivatives.

Ovens should be preheated to the specified temperature – if using a fan-assisted oven, follow the manufacturer's instructions for adjusting the time and the temperature.

The heat and flavour of fresh, dried and ground chillies, curry pastes and spices varies enormously, so always add small amounts first, then taste and adjust the amounts as required.

Always take care when using chillies. After preparation, wash your hands, knives and chopping board thoroughly and never let any part of the chilli get near your eyes.

Preparing fresh chillies. For a very hot result, break off the stalk and wash the chilli under cold running water. For a milder flavour, remove the seeds: cut the chilli in half lengthways with a sharp knife. Scrape out the seeds with the point of a knife and cut away the fleshy white ribs from each half.

Contents

Introduction

'Curry' is an anglicized Indian word, derived, it is thought, either from *kari*, a Tamil word for sauce, or from *karhai*, a widely used Indian cooking vessel. Originally it meant food stewed with liquid and various spices and other flavourings, which cook together to form a sauce – an Oriental casserole, in fact. Now, 'curry' has taken on a wider meaning, signifying a generally hot, sometimes fiery dish, richly flavoured with spices and herbs.

Thus, in this book, there are recipes for soups and starters and for fish and shellfish dishes alongside the meat and poultry stews and vegetable dishes which are what we usually think of when we use the word 'curry'.

Not all curries come from India, as a glance at this book will show, for spiced dishes are popular in the cuisines of Thailand, Malaysia and Indonesia. Because both the Chinese and the Indians have had an influence on South-east Asian cooking, these curries tend to be less obviously 'Indian' and contain milder flavours as well as the hotter ones more often associated with curries.

In India itself there have been numerous outside influences on the country's cooking. The subtly spiced

curries from the north, especially Kashmir, owe much to the sophistication of the cooks at the luxurious courts of the Mughal emperors, who conquered northern India from Persia. The British, too, had an influence on Indian cooking: Mulligatawny Soup (see page 10) was invented to suit British Army demands for a soup course at dinner. Balti dishes are both Indian and British, for Balti is a type of Kashmiri curry from Baltistan, in Pakistan, which was developed in the Midlands of Britain by immigrants after the Second World War. Pakoras (the Indian vegetable fritters on pages 8 and 13) – an exotic nibble to serve with drinks before dinner – are a comparatively recent import to Britain.

SPICES IN CURRY COOKING

While there are numerous distinctly flavoured ingredients which recur frequently in curry making, such as coconut, ginger, onions and tamarind, no dish can be called a curry if it does not contain a selection of spices. Many spices are used in making curries, all of them with a distinctive flavour to offer – which is why there are so many curries in India, for there is almost no limit to the possible combinations of spices. Balti curries, served in their distinctive two-handled metal pan, are subtle rather than fiery, and simple to improvise, for they are based on ingredients found in most kitchens, such as onions, tomatoes, cumin and coriander.

It is best to keep only small quantities of frequently used spices in the kitchen, storing them in a cool, dry place and using them within six months, for a stale spice has little to offer any curry. An electric coffee grinder, kept specially for the purpose, makes grinding whole spices easy.

Among the most widely used spices in curry-making are:

ANISEED: small seeds with a liquorice flavour, widely used in India to flavour confectionery and chutneys.

ASAFOETIDA: pale yellow spice with a strong and distinctive flavour which helps enhance other flavours in a recipe, particularly in Indian bean and lentil dishes.
BLACK ONION SEEDS (Kalonji): small black seeds with an appealingly earthy flavour, used in Bengal in fish and vegetable dishes and in other parts of India in pickles.
CARDAMOM (pods and seeds): highly aromatic green pods widely used in Indian cookery. If they are used whole in a recipe, they should be removed before serving; the seeds (best removed from the pods as you need them, not bought in packets) are left in the dish.
CHILLIES (fresh red and green chillies; dried red chillies; also CAYENNE PEPPER): chillies, brought to India from Central America, give curries their fiery heat. If fresh or dried chillies are not available, cayenne pepper (called red chilli powder in Indian groceries) makes a good substitute. A chilli is less fiery if the seeds are removed from the pod. When handling chillies never touch your face or rub your eyes until you have washed your hands. Chilli paste and chilli sauce are also available.
CINNAMON: a spice from the bark of a small evergreen tree. This is used in Indian cookery, in savoury meat and rice dishes, and in sweets. It is used in the form of sticks, rather than as a powder. The sticks are used whole or in large pieces and should be removed from a dish before it is served.
CLOVES: a strongly aromatic spice used in Indian meat and rice dishes. Usually used whole, not ground, and removed from the dish before serving.
CORIANDER SEEDS: an essential and distinctive curry flavouring. The round, light brown seeds are used whole or ground in meat and vegetable dishes. Chopped coriander roots are used in Thai cooking, while fresh coriander leaves are popular in India as a flavouring for all kinds of curry.
CUMIN: these seeds, available in both black and white and also in ground form, are an important spice in Indian cooking.
FENNEL SEEDS: these have a mildly aniseed flavour and are used in meat and vegetable dishes.
FENUGREEK: seeds with a strong and bittersweet flavour, used sparingly in curry powders.
MUSTARD SEEDS: tiny, round seeds, usually described as black, though they are, in fact, reddish-brown. They take on a deliciously nutty flavour when scattered into hot oil at the beginning of a recipe.
NUTMEG: fragrant spice, best used freshly grated, for which special small nutmeg graters are obtainable.
SAFFRON (threads and powder): an expensive spice, used in dishes for special occasions both for its lovely yellow colour and its aroma.
TURMERIC: a spice with a mild, earthy flavour, widely used in Indian cooking to impart a good deep yellow colour.

DRY-FRYING SPICES

Dry-frying, or roasting, spices brings out their distinctive flavours. It is usual in Indian cooking to dry-fry several whole spices at once, depending on what will be needed in the recipe being prepared. Use a heavy-based frying pan and put all the spices in an even layer into the pan set over a moderate heat. Stir-fry the spices for about 5 minutes, until they are a shade or two darker and beginning to give off a delicious aroma. Allow the spices to cool, then grind them in a mortar or an electric coffee grinder.

SOME BASIC RECIPES

These recipes include basic mixtures and curry pastes used in a variety of dishes and two garnishes with the distinct flavour of Oriental cooking.

COCONUT MILK AND CREAM

Mix 400 g/13 oz grated or desiccated coconut with 900 ml/1½ pints milk in a saucepan, bring to the boil, lower the heat and simmer, stirring occasionally, until the mixture has reduced by one third. Strain, extracting as much liquid as possible. Pour the strained milk into a bowl and chill in the refrigerator. When it is cold, skim off the thicker 'cream' that rises to the surface. The remaining liquid is the coconut milk.

Coconut milk is particularly good with shellfish, as in the recipe for Siamese Pineapple and Mussel Curry (see page 20).

THAI RED CURRY PASTE

Deseed 6 dried red chillies and soak them in water for 10 minutes. Drain well and chop roughly. Place in a food processor and work to a smooth paste

MAKING PAKORAS (INDIAN VEGETABLE FRITTERS)

1 To make the fritter batter, the flour is sifted into a bowl, then salt and chilli powder are added and water or yogurt are beaten in. The batter is left to stand until it is very thick, before any herbs and spices are added.

2 The prepared vegetable pieces, such as onion rings, spinach, chopped courgettes and cooked sliced potatoes, are dipped into the batter and turned in it so that they are thoroughly coated. The oil for deep-frying is heated in a heavy saucepan or deep-fat fryer.

3 The pakoras are fried in the hot oil, a few at a time, until they are golden and crisp. When cooked, they are lifted out with a slotted spoon and dried on kitchen paper. Pakoras are best served warm, with a chutney or hot sauce.

with 2 tablespoons chopped lemon grass, 1 tablespoon chopped shallot, 1 tablespoon chopped garlic, 1 tablespoon chopped coriander stem, 1 teaspoon chopped galangal, 2 teaspoons coriander seeds, 1 teaspoon cumin seeds, 6 white peppercorns, 1 teaspoon cumin seeds, 1 teaspoon salt and 1 teaspoon shrimp paste. Store in a screwtop jar in the refrigerator for up to 3 weeks.

This curry paste is a splendid addition to recipes as diverse as Laksa (see page 12) and Thai Red Beef Curry (see page 55).

Garlic Mixture

Put 2 tablespoons crushed garlic, 2 tablespoons chopped coriander stem and ½ teaspoon pepper into a mortar and pound to a paste. This pungent mixture gives an extra piquancy to fish dishes such as Thai Grilled Mullet (see page 16).

Thai Green Curry Paste

Remove the stems and seeds from 6 dried green chillies. Place them in a food processor and work to a smooth paste with 3 tablespoons finely chopped spring onions, 1 tablespoon chopped garlic, 1 tablespoon chopped lemon grass, 1 tablespoon shrimp paste, 1 teaspoon ground galangal (laos powder), 1 teaspoon caraway seeds, 2 teaspoons coriander seeds, 1 teaspoon finely grated lemon rind and 1 teaspoon salt. Green curry paste can be stored in a screwtop jar in the refrigerator for up to 3 weeks.

This curry paste is an excellent base for recipes including poultry. In this book, it is used in Green Duck Curry (see page 28) and Thai Green Chicken Curry (see page 34). Although it is not as fiery as red curry paste, it is still a hot spice mixture.

Fried Onion Rings

Heat about 300 ml/½ pint vegetable oil in a wok or deep-fat fryer until hot but not smoking, add 1 large, thinly sliced onion and deep-fry for 3–4 minutes, until golden brown. Remove from the pan with a slotted spoon and drain on kitchen paper. Serve them hot or at room temperature. These Fried Onion

Rings make an eye-appealing garnish and are particularly good served with rice dishes, such as Pilau Rice (see page 90).

FRIED ONION FLAKES

Measure out 50 g/2 oz dried onion flakes. Heat about 300 ml/½ pint vegetable oil in a deep-fat fryer to 180–190°C/350–375°F. Put a quarter of the onion flakes in a metal sieve and lower them into the hot oil, frying them for a few seconds until they are golden brown. Remove from the fat and drain on kitchen paper. Repeat with the remaining onion flakes. Cool, then store in an airtight container. Onion flakes will keep for 3–4 weeks.

The dried onion flakes for this Indonesian garnish are available from Asian grocers and most large supermarkets.

GARNISHING CURRIES

A crisply prepared, single-colour garnish is ideal for curries, which is why fresh herbs are among the most popular garnishes in Oriental cooking. One of the best garnish herbs is coriander, its broad, brightly green leaves standing out well against the colours and ingredients of most curries. Other often-used herbs are parsley (especially the flat-leafed variety), mint and Thai basil.

Chillies are used in various forms as garnishes. Small dried red chillies are often used whole as a garnish, while fresh red chillies may be cut into a flower (for dishes in which the Chinese influence is strong) or sliced into rings. Chilli powder is also often used as a garnish.

Fruits and vegetables making good garnishes include lemons and limes (cut into slices or wedges), onions (thin slices served either raw or fried, as in Fried Onion Rings, on page 8) and spring onions (cut into rings for curries, rather than into the spring onion tassels used in Chinese cooking). Red and green peppers make a good garnish, too, usually served thinly sliced. Not a garnish as such, but essential accompaniments to curries, are chapati and other breads, chutneys and cooling raitas.

MAKING CHAPATI (UNLEAVENED BREAD)

1 The flour and salt are mixed with water to a soft, supple dough, which is kneaded for 10 minutes. It is then put in a bowl, covered and left to rise in a cool place for 30 minutes. The dough is knocked back and kneaded thoroughly and divided into 12 pieces.

2 Each piece of dough is put on a lightly floured surface and rolled out with a rolling pin into a thin round pancake.

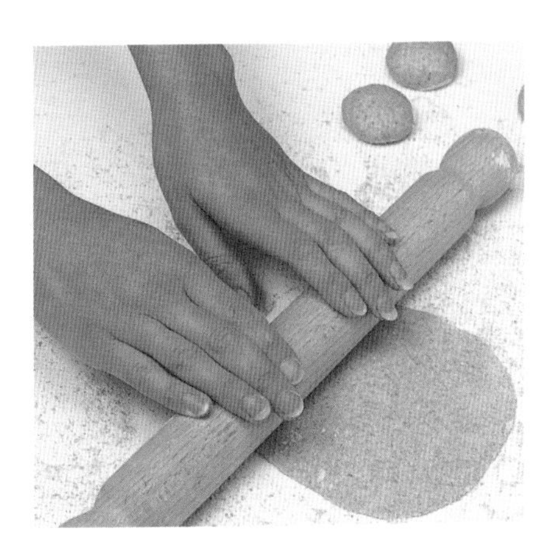

3 A griddle or heavy frying pan is lightly greased and set over a moderate heat. The chapatis are cooked, one at a time, being pressed down with a fish slice. When blisters appear on the chapati it is turned over and cooked on the other side until lightly coloured. They are served warm, brushed with a little butter and folded into quarters.

Soups and Starters

Mulligatawny Soup

Mulligatawny has no history in India before the British Raj – this spicy soup was simply an invention to satisfy the demands of army officers for a soup course at dinner. The literal translation of the Tamil word 'mulligatawny' is pepper water.

50 g/2 oz dried tamarind
1.2 litres/2 pints beef stock
50 g/2 oz ghee or butter
1 large onion, sliced
2 garlic cloves, sliced
1 teaspoon ground ginger
2 teaspoons pepper
2 teaspoons ground coriander
½ teaspoon ground fenugreek
½ teaspoon chilli powder
1½ teaspoons turmeric
1½ teaspoons salt
thinly sliced red and green peppers, to garnish

1 Put the dried tamarind into a saucepan, add just enough of the beef stock to cover, then bring to the boil. Remove the pan from the heat, cover and leave the tamarind to soak for 4 hours.

2 Melt the ghee or butter in a wok or heavy-based saucepan, add the onion and garlic and fry gently for about 4–5 minutes until soft.

3 Add the ginger, pepper, ground coriander, fenugreek, chilli powder, turmeric and salt and fry for 3 minutes, stirring constantly. Stir in the remaining beef stock. Strain the tamarind liquid through a wire sieve over a small bowl, pressing to extract as much liquid as possible. Add the tamarind juice to the wok and simmer for 15 minutes. Taste and adjust the seasoning before serving, garnished with the sliced peppers. Serve hot.

Serves 4
Preparation time: 10 minutes, plus soaking
Cooking time: 25 minutes

Laksa

The English translation of this Malaysian dish is Rice Noodles with Curried Chicken Soup. Despite its name, it really is a meal in itself.

- 6 tablespoons vegetable oil
- 250 g/8 oz pressed beancurd, cubed
- 2 red onions, finely chopped
- 3 garlic cloves, finely chopped
- 4 Brazil nuts, finely grated
- 2 teaspoons ground cumin
- 1 tablespoon ground coriander
- ½ teaspoon turmeric
- 1 red chilli, deseeded and chopped
- 1 green chilli, deseeded and chopped
- ½ teaspoon shrimp paste
- 2 tablespoons Thai red curry paste (see pages 7–8)
- 1 litre/1¾ pints coconut milk (see page 7)
- 1 tablespoon soft brown sugar
- 375 g/12 oz cooked chicken breasts, shredded
- 125 g/4 oz bean sprouts
- 1 tablespoon chopped fresh coriander
- 250 g/8 oz dried rice vermicelli or noodles
- salt and pepper

TO GARNISH:

- 2 fresh red chillies, chopped
- fresh coriander leaves
- 3 spring onions, sliced

1 Heat 2 tablespoons of the oil in a wok. Fry the beancurd in the oil, in 2 batches, turning it frequently. Cook each batch for 5 minutes until crisp and golden, then remove with a slotted spoon, place to drain on kitchen paper and set aside.

2 Heat 2 more tablespoons of oil in the wok, add the onion and garlic and fry over a gentle heat, stirring frequently, for 5 minutes until softened.

3 Add the Brazil nuts, the ground cumin, coriander and turmeric, the red and green chillies and the shrimp and curry pastes to the wok. Stir well to mix and fry for a further 2 minutes.

4 Stir in the coconut milk and sugar and season generously with salt and pepper. Bring the curried coconut milk to the boil, then reduce the heat and simmer gently for 6 minutes. Taste and adjust the seasoning if necessary.

5 Heat the remaining oil in a frying pan, add the chicken and stir-fry for 6 minutes until golden. Add the bean sprouts and chopped coriander and stir-fry for a further 1 minute.

6 Place the vermicelli or noodles in a bowl and pour boiling water over them to cover completely. Allow to stand for 5 minutes, then drain well.

7 To serve, divide the vermicelli among 4 soup bowls. Place a quarter of the fried beancurd and a quarter of the chicken and bean sprout mixture on top of each portion of noodles. Ladle over the hot curry sauce and scatter over the suggested garnishes. Serve immediately.

Serves 4

Preparation time: about 20 minutes

Cooking time: 40 minutes

Pakoras

These spicy nibbles, from northern India, can be served as a starter or with drinks. Discard the seeds from the chillies for a less spicy version.

- **125 g/4 oz gram or chickpea flour**
- **1 teaspoon salt**
- **½ teaspoon chilli powder**
- **about 150 ml/¼ pint water or yogurt**
- **2 green chillies, finely chopped**
- **1 tablespoon finely chopped fresh coriander**
- **1 teaspoon melted butter or ghee**
- **2 onions, cut into rings**
- **oil, for deep-frying**
- **8 small fresh spinach leaves**
- **2–3 potatoes, parboiled and sliced**

1 Sift the flour, salt and chilli powder into a bowl. Stir in sufficient water or yogurt to make a thick batter and beat well until smooth. Cover the bowl and leave to stand for 30 minutes.
2 Stir the chillies and coriander into the batter, then add the melted butter or ghee. Drop in the onion rings to coat thickly with batter.
3 Heat the oil in a deep pan, add the onion rings and deep-fry until crisp and golden. Remove from the pan with a slotted spoon, drain on kitchen paper and keep warm.
4 Dip the spinach leaves into the batter and deep-fry in the same way, adding more oil to the pan if necessary.
5 Finally, repeat the process with the potato slices. Serve hot, with a chilli sauce, if liked.

Serves 4
Preparation time: 15–20 minutes, plus standing
Cooking time: about 25 minutes

Prawn and Egg Sambal

- 500 g/1 lb tiger prawn tails
- 4 hard-boiled eggs, shelled and quartered
- 300 ml/½ pint coconut milk (see page 7)
- 1 small onion, finely chopped
- 1 garlic clove, crushed
- 1 fresh green chilli, deseeded and chopped
- juice of ½ lemon
- pinch of chilli powder
- ½ teaspoon salt

TO GARNISH:

- 50 g/2 oz cooked green peas
- chopped fresh coriander leaves

1 Arrange the prawns and eggs in a shallow serving dish, then cover and chill in the refrigerator while you make the sauce.

2 Place the coconut milk, onion, garlic, chilli, lemon juice, chilli powder and salt in a food processor and purée until smooth and evenly mixed. Pour the mixture over the prawns and eggs, then cover and chill until required.

3 Serve the sambal well chilled, garnished with the peas and chopped fresh coriander, and accompanied by poppadoms if you like.

Serves 4

Preparation time: 15 minutes, plus chilling

Vegetable Samosas

PASTRY:

- **125 g/4 oz plain flour**
- **¼ teaspoon salt**
- **25 g/1 oz ghee or butter**
- **2–3 tablespoons water**

FILLING:

- **1 tablespoon oil**
- **1 teaspoon mustard seeds**
- **1 small onion, finely chopped**
- **2 green chillies, minced**
- **¼ teaspoon turmeric**
- **1 teaspoon finely chopped fresh root ginger**
- **salt**
- **125 g/4 oz frozen peas**
- **125 g/4 oz cooked potatoes, diced**
- **½ tablespoon chopped fresh coriander**
- **1 tablespoon lemon juice**
- **oil, for deep-frying**

1 First make the pastry. Sift the flour and salt into a bowl. Rub in the ghee or butter until the mixture resembles breadcrumbs. Add the water and knead to a very smooth dough. Cover and chill while preparing the filling.

2 Heat the oil in a large saucepan and add the mustard seeds. Leave for a few seconds until they start to pop, then add the onion and fry for about 5 minutes until golden.

3 Add the chillies, turmeric, ginger and salt to taste and fry for 3 minutes; if the mixture starts sticking add ½ tablespoon water and stir well. Add the peas, stir well and cook for 2 minutes. Add the potatoes and coriander, stir well and cook for 1 minute. Stir in the lemon juice. Cool slightly.

4 Divide the pastry into 8 pieces. Dust with flour and roll each piece into a thin round, then cut each round in half. Fold each half into a cone and brush the seam with water to seal.

5 Fill the cone with a spoonful of filling (do not overfill), dampen the top edge and seal firmly. Heat the oil and deep-fry the samosas until crisp and golden. Serve hot or warm with a raita.

Serves 4

Preparation time: 15 minutes, plus chilling

Cooking time: about 30 minutes

Fish and Shellfish

Thai Grilled Mullet

1 medium grey mullet, cleaned
½ tablespoon garlic mixture (see page 8)
½ onion, chopped
5 mushrooms, wiped and sliced
2 tablespoons shredded root ginger
1 celery stick, sliced
1 teaspoon pepper
1 tablespoon tao chiew (salted soya bean flavouring)
1 tablespoon oyster sauce
250 ml/8 fl oz fish stock or water

TO SERVE:

1 lettuce, separated into leaves
3 lemon slices

1 Place the fish on a wooden board and score the skin 2–3 times with a sharp knife to allow the sauce to be absorbed during cooking. Rub the fish with garlic mixture, pressing it well into the cuts. Transfer the fish to a shallow heatproof dish.

2 In a bowl, mix all the remaining ingredients well and pour over the fish. Place the fish under a preheated grill and cook for 20 minutes, turning the fish over halfway through the cooking time.

3 Just before serving, arrange a bed of lettuce on a shallow serving dish. Carefully transfer the fish to the dish, pour over the vegetable sauce and garnish with the lemon slices. Serve immediately.

Serves 4
Preparation time: 10–15 minutes
Cooking time: 20 minutes

Chilli Prawns with Cherry Tomatoes

Raw tiger prawn tails are available at good fishmongers and the fresh fish counters of large supermarkets. They are expensive but well worth it, for they are large, juicy, and full of flavour – far superior to the ubiquitous pale pink cooked variety.

- **3 tablespoons vegetable oil**
- **1 small onion, finely chopped**
- **2.5 cm/1 inch piece of fresh root ginger, peeled and finely chopped**
- **2 garlic cloves, crushed**
- **1–2 fresh chillies or 1–2 teaspoons chilli powder, according to taste**
- **375 g/12 oz raw tiger prawn tails, defrosted and dried thoroughly if frozen, peeled**
- **6–8 cherry tomatoes, halved**
- **2 tablespoons tomato purée**
- **1 tablespoon red or white wine vinegar**
- **pinch of caster sugar**
- **½ teaspoon salt**
- **sprigs of coriander, to garnish**

1 Heat a wok until hot. Add the oil and heat over moderate heat until hot. Add the onion, ginger, garlic and chillies or chilli powder and stir-fry for 2–3 minutes or until softened, taking care not to let the ingredients brown.

2 Add the prawns, increase the heat to high and stir-fry for 1–2 minutes or until they turn pink. Add the tomatoes, tomato purée, wine vinegar, sugar and salt. Increase the heat to high and stir-fry for several minutes or until the mixture is thick, taking care not to let the cherry tomatoes lose their shape. Taste and add more salt if necessary. Serve at once, garnished with sprigs of coriander.

Serves 4

Preparation time: 10 minutes

Cooking time: 10–15 minutes

Prawn Chilli Fry

This is a quick and easy way to transform a packet of cooked peeled prawns from the supermarket into a quick and delicious spicy supper dish. It has a less subtle flavour than Chilli Prawns with Cherry Tomatoes on page 18, but costs considerably less.

- **3 tablespoons oil**
- **3 onions, sliced**
- **2 green chillies, chopped**
- **2.5 cm/1 inch piece of fresh root ginger, chopped**
- **½ teaspoon chilli powder**
- **½ teaspoon turmeric**
- **salt**
- **375 g/12 oz cooked peeled prawns**

1 Heat the oil in a large frying pan, add the onions and fry gently for 5 minutes until soft and golden. Add the chillies, ginger, chilli powder, turmeric and salt to taste and fry for 2 minutes.

2 Add the prawns and cook, uncovered, for about 3 minutes or until all the moisture has evaporated. Serve immediately with boiled or fried rice.

Serves 4

Preparation time: 5 minutes

Cooking time: about 10 minutes

Siamese Pineapple and Mussel Curry

Sometimes known as holy basil, Thai basil is an Asian variety of popular European herb sweet basil. It has small green leaves and purple stems and flowers, and its flavour is a mixture of sweet basil and aniseed. It is found in Thai and Chinese shops, but sweet basil can be substituted if it is not available. Galangal is a spice popular in South-East Asia which looks, and tastes, rather like ginger.

- **1 kg/2 lb fresh mussels**
- **2 stalks of lemon grass, roughly chopped**
- **20 Thai basil leaves**
- **2 tablespoons groundnut oil**
- **2 tablespoons Thai red curry paste (see page 7)**
- **5 cm/2 inch piece of fresh galangal, finely chopped**
- **1 large green chilli, thinly sliced**
- **kaffir lime leaves, finely chopped**
- **200 ml/7 fl oz coconut milk (see page 7)**
- **1 tablespoon Thai fish sauce (nam pla)**
- **1 teaspoon palm sugar or soft brown sugar**
- **175 g/6 oz peeled fresh pineapple, cut into bite-sized pieces**
- **sprigs of Thai basil, to garnish (optional)**

1 Scrub the mussels with a stiff brush and scrape off the beards and barnacles with a sharp knife. Wash well in cold water and discard any open mussels.

2 Pour about 2.5 cm/1 inch water into a large saucepan, add the chopped lemon grass and Thai basil and bring the water to the boil. Tip in the mussels, cover the pan and steam the mussels for 3–4 minutes or until they have opened and are cooked. Drain the mussels, discarding the lemon grass, Thai basil and any mussels which have not opened. Set the mussels on one side while preparing the sauce.

3 Heat the oil in a heavy-based saucepan, add the curry paste, galangal, chilli and lime leaves and fry over gentle heat, stirring, for about 4 minutes until fragrant. Stir in the coconut milk, fish sauce and sugar and cook for 1 further minute.

4 Reserve a few mussels in their shells for garnish and remove the remaining mussels from their shells. Add the shelled mussels and pineapple to the curry sauce. Stir gently and cook for 2–3 minutes to heat through. Serve hot, garnished with the reserved mussels and Thai basil, if using.

Serves 4

Preparation time: 30 minutes
Cooking time: 10–15 minutes

Fish Fillets in Spicy Turmeric and Coconut Sauce

- 4 thick haddock fillets (taken from the centre of the fish), skinned
- juice of 2 limes
- 2 teaspoons turmeric
- 1 small onion, roughly chopped
- 1–2 garlic cloves, roughly chopped
- 2 fresh chillies, deseeded and roughly chopped
- 2 teaspoons ground coriander
- 1 teaspoon ground galangal (laos powder)
- about 300 ml/½ pint vegetable oil, for shallow-frying
- 100 g/3½ oz creamed coconut, roughly chopped
- 1 teaspoon soft brown sugar
- ½ teaspoon salt

TO GARNISH:

- lime wedges
- chopped red chillies

1 Arrange the haddock fillets in a single layer in a shallow dish. Pour over the lime juice, then rub the turmeric into the flesh. Cover and leave to stand for about 20 minutes.

2 Meanwhile, place the onion, garlic, chillies, coriander and ground galangal in a food processor or blender and work to a paste, adding a little water if necessary. Set aside.

3 Heat the oil in a wok over moderate heat until hot but not smoking. With a fish slice, lower 2 of the haddock fillets into the hot oil and shallow-fry for 5 minutes, taking care to keep them whole. Remove with the fish slice and drain on kitchen paper. Shallow-fry and drain the 2 remaining fillets in the same way.

4 Pour off all but 2 tablespoons oil from the wok. Add the spice paste and stir-fry over a gentle heat for 3–4 minutes. Add the chopped coconut, then pour in 300 ml/½ pint boiling water and stir constantly until the coconut is dissolved. Add the sugar and salt and bring to the boil, stirring, then lower the heat and simmer until thickened, stirring frequently.

5 Return the haddock fillets to the wok and carefully spoon over the sauce, taking care not to break the pieces of fish. Heat through very gently, then transfer to warmed plates with a fish slice. Spoon the coconut sauce over and around the fish and garnish with lime wedges and chopped red chillies. Serve at once.

Serves 4

Preparation time: 10 minutes, plus standing

Cooking time: 25–30 minutes

Steamed Tuna Fish Curry in Banana Leaves

This is a fresh-tasting curry from southern India. It looks most attractive served on banana leaves, which can be bought at ethnic markets. If they are not available, wrap the tuna steaks in a double thickness of buttered greaseproof paper for steaming.

- **4 x 150 g/5 oz fresh tuna steaks**
- **juice of 1 lime**
- **4 large pieces of banana leaf**

GREEN CURRY PASTE:

- **1 tablespoon cumin seeds**
- **2 tablespoons coriander seeds**
- **3 large green chillies, deseeded and chopped**
- **25 g/1 oz fresh mint leaves**
- **5 cm/2 inch piece of fresh root ginger, grated**
- **4 garlic cloves, crushed**
- **25 g/1 oz caster sugar**
- **½ teaspoon salt**
- **75 g/3 oz desiccated coconut**
- **50 ml/2 fl oz malt vinegar**

TO GARNISH:

- **1 onion, cut into rings**
- **2 green chillies, deseeded and cut into rings**
- **sprigs of mint**
- **lime wedges**

1 Place the tuna steaks in a shallow, non-metallic dish and pour over the lime juice. Cover and set aside to marinate while making the curry paste.

2 To make the green curry paste, place the cumin and coriander seeds in a food processor or blender and process briefly. Add the chillies, mint, ginger and garlic, and work for 1 minute to produce a paste. Add the sugar, salt, coconut and vinegar, and blend again until all the ingredients are thoroughly combined.

3 Lay the pieces of banana leaf or buttered greaseproof paper on a flat surface. Remove the tuna from the lime juice and place a steak in the centre of each banana leaf. Spread the green curry paste over the tuna, completely covering the fish. Wrap up the banana leaves to enclose the pieces of fish, and fasten securely with wooden cocktail sticks.

4 Steam the fish over boiling water for 18–20 minutes, or until the fish flakes when tested with the point of a knife.

5 Garnish the fish with onion, chilli rings and mint springs, and serve with wedges of lime.

Serves 4

Preparation time: about 10 minutes

Cooking time: 20 minutes

Fish with Ginger and Soya

- 2 medium grey mullet or mackerel, cleaned
- oil, for deep-frying
- 2 tablespoons vegetable oil
- 2 garlic cloves, crushed
- 2 tablespoons shredded root ginger
- 1 tablespoon tao chiew (salted soya bean flavouring)
- 1 tablespoon sugar
- 1 teaspoon Thai fish sauce (nam pla)
- ½ teaspoon pepper
- 250 ml/8 fl oz fish stock or water
- 5 spring onions, sliced

TO GARNISH:

- fresh coriander leaves
- strips of red chilli

1 Cut the fish into large chunks and dry on kitchen paper. Heat the oil in a wok or deep-fat fryer and deep-fry the fish for 10–15 minutes until golden brown. Remove the fish with a slotted spoon and drain on kitchen paper.

2 Heat the vegetable oil in a saucepan large enough to hold the fish chunks in a single layer. Stir in the garlic and cook until pale gold in colour. Add the ginger, tao chiew, sugar, fish sauce and pepper and stir well.

3 Stir in the stock and bring the liquid to the boil. Add the fried fish and spring onions, lower the heat and simmer for 10 minutes.

4 Serve hot, garnished with coriander leaves and strips of red chilli.

Serves 4

Preparation time: 10 minutes

Cooking time: about 30 minutes

Fish Curry with Coconut Milk

The Indian name for this curry from southern India is Fish Molee.

- **750 g/1½ lb cod fillet, skinned**
- **2 tablespoons plain flour**
- **4 tablespoons oil**
- **2 onions, sliced**
- **2 garlic cloves, crushed**
- **1 teaspoon turmeric**
- **4 green chillies, deseeded and finely chopped**
- **2 tablespoons lemon juice**
- **175 ml/6 fl oz thick coconut milk (see page 7)**
- **salt**

TO GARNISH:

- **slices of red chilli**
- **snipped chives**

1 Cut the fish into 4 and coat with the flour. Heat the oil in a frying pan, and fry the fish quickly on both sides. Lift out with a slotted spoon and set aside.
2 Add the onion and garlic to the pan and fry for about 5 minutes until soft and golden. Add the turmeric, chillies, lemon juice, coconut milk and salt to taste and simmer, uncovered, for 10 minutes or until thickened.
3 Add the fish and any juices, spoon over the sauce and cook gently for 2–3 minutes, until tender. Garnish with chillies and chives and serve at once.

Serves 4
Preparation time: 10 minutes
Cooking time: about 20 minutes

Assam Fish Curry

Assam means sour in Malay and usually implies that tamarind pulp is used in the cooking, for its distinctive, tangy flavour.

- **4 tablespoons vegetable oil**
- **3 tablespoons tamarind pulp, soaked in 250 ml/8 fl oz boiling water for 10 minutes**
- **2 tomatoes, quartered**
- **2 baby aubergines, weighing about 50 g/2 oz each, quartered**
- **2 large fresh red chillies, quartered lengthways and deseeded**
- **1 tablespoon soft brown sugar**
- **½ teaspoon salt**
- **625 g/1¼ lb skinless haddock or halibut, cut into 5 cm/2 inch pieces**

SPICE PASTE:

- **5 small dried chillies soaked in cold water for 10 minutes, then deseeded and chopped**
- **8 shallots, chopped**
- **3 stalks of lemon grass, chopped**
- **2 fresh red chillies, deseeded and chopped**
- **2.5 cm/1 inch piece of fresh galangal, chopped**
- **2 teaspoon dried shrimp paste**
- **1 teaspoon turmeric**
- **5 candlenuts or macadamia nuts (optional)**

1 To make the spice paste, put the dried chillies, shallots, lemon grass, red chillies, galangal, shrimp paste, turmeric and candlenuts or macadamia nuts, if using, in a food processor or blender and work to a thick paste. Heat the oil in a large saucepan, add the spice paste and fry over gentle heat, stirring constantly, for about 5 minutes until softened.

2 Strain the tamarind pulp through a sieve, pressing it against the sieve to extract as much tamarind flavour as possible. Discard the pulp and add the strained tamarind liquid to the pan with the tomatoes, aubergines and chillies. Bring to the boil, then reduce the heat, cover the pan and simmer gently for 12 minutes.

3 Add the sugar, salt and prepared fish to the pan and stir gently to coat the fish in the sauce. Cover the pan and cook the curry over a gentle heat for a further 7 minutes or until the fish is cooked through. Taste and adjust the seasoning if necessary. Serve the curry hot with plain boiled rice.

Serves 4

Preparation time: about 20 minutes, plus soaking

Cooking time: 25–30 minutes

VARIATION

Assam Squid Curry

Use the same ingredients as in the main recipe but replacing the fish with 375 g/12 oz small squid, cleaned but left whole. Follow the method in the main recipe until the final step when the squid is added to the pan. Cook the squid for about 5 minutes, stirring occasionally, leaving the pan uncovered at this stage.

Spicy Fried Fishcakes

- 500 g/1 lb cod fillet, skinned and cut into chunks
- 3 tablespoons Thai red curry paste (see page 7)
- 1 egg
- 3 tablespoons Thai fish sauce (nam pla)
- 75 g/3 oz French beans, finely chopped
- 1 tablespoon finely shredded makrut (citrus) leaves
- oil, for shallow frying

1 Combine the fish and the curry paste in a food processor or blender, and process until the fish is finely chopped. Alternatively, use a pestle and mortar.

2 Transfer the fish mixture to a bowl and add the egg and nam pla. Knead to make a stiff mixture. Work in the French beans and makrut leaves in the same way.

3 Form the mixture into 16–20 balls and flatten each one to a round about 1 cm/½ inch thick. Heat the oil in a large frying pan, add the fishcakes and fry for 4–5 minutes on each side over medium heat. Do not allow the fishcakes to overcook, or they will dry out.

4 Lift the fishcakes out of the pan with a slotted spoon and drain on kitchen paper, transfer to a serving plate and serve hot with a salad.

Serves 4

Preparation time: 15 minutes

Cooking time: about 10 minutes

Chicken and Duck

Green Duck Curry

2–2.5 kg/4–5 lb duckling with giblets
coarse salt, for sprinkling
500 ml/17 fl oz thick coconut milk (see page 7)
500 ml/17 fl oz thin coconut milk (see page 7)
4 kaffir lime leaves, more for garnish
2½ tablespoons Thai green curry paste (see page 8)
2–3 fresh green chillies, deseeded and sliced
Thai fish sauce (nam pla), to taste
sliced red chillies, to garnish

1 Dry the duck thoroughly with kitchen paper. Sprinkle the skin generously with coarse salt. Set aside for 15 minutes.
2 Brush off the salt and chop the duck into 5 cm/2 inch pieces. Heat a wok or frying pan over medium-high heat. Add a few pieces of duck and brown them thoroughly. Remove with a slotted spoon and drain on kitchen paper. Brown the remaining duck pieces in the same way. Discard the rendered fat from the wok and wipe it clean.
3 Reduce the heat to moderate. Skim the coconut cream from the top of the thick coconut milk and bring to the boil in the wok, then add the lime leaves and curry paste. Reduce the heat and cook, stirring constantly, until the oil begins to separate. Add the duck pieces, turn to cover evenly with the sauce then cook gently for 5 minutes.
4 Add the thick and thin coconut milks, bring just to the boil, then reduce the heat to very low. Simmer, stirring occasionally, for about 1–1¼ hours until the duck is tender.
5 Remove from the heat, transfer to a bowl and allow to cool. Cover and chill overnight.
6 Skin the excess fat from the curry, then return to the wok, stir in the chillies and season with Thai fish sauce. Simmer for 5 minutes or until heated through, then transfer to a warmed serving dish, garnish with sliced red chillies and shredded lime leaves and serve immediately.

Serves 4–6
Preparation time: 15 minutes, plus standing and chilling
Cooking time: 1½–1¾ hours

Oriental Chicken with Turmeric

Macadamia nuts are noted for their rich flavour and waxy texture. Be sure to buy the unsalted ones for this recipe. Serai or sereh powder is dried lemon grass, a convenient way of adding this lovely citrus flavour to Oriental curries and stir-fries. If you are lucky enough to be able to get fresh lemon grass, you can use it instead of the serai powder and lemon rind in this dish. You will need 1 stalk of lemon grass, bruised.

- **100 g/3½ oz creamed coconut, roughly chopped**
- **50 g/2 oz macadamia nuts, roughly chopped**
- **1 garlic clove, roughly chopped**
- **3 tablespoons vegetable oil**
- **1 onion, finely chopped**
- **8 boneless chicken thighs, skinned and cut into large chunks**
- **1 tablespoon turmeric**
- **1 teaspoon serai powder**
- **thinly pared rind and juice of 1 lemon**
- **salt and pepper**
- **flat leaf parsley, to garnish**

1 First make the coconut milk. Put the chopped coconut into a measuring jug, pour in boiling water up to the 300 ml/½ pint mark and stir until the coconut is dissolved. Set aside.
2 Pound half of the macadamia nuts to a paste with the garlic using a pestle and mortar. Heat a wok until hot. Add the oil and heat over moderate heat until hot. Add the onion together with the nut and garlic paste and stir-fry for 2–3 minutes or until the onion is softened, taking care not to let the ingredients brown.
3 Add the chicken pieces, increase the heat to high and stir-fry for 1–2 minutes or until the chicken is lightly coloured on all sides. Stir in the turmeric and serai powder and season to taste with salt and pepper. Add the coconut milk and bring to the boil, stirring constantly.
4 Lower the heat, add the lemon rind and juice and simmer for about 10 minutes or until the chicken is tender and the sauce thickened, stirring frequently to prevent sticking. Remove and discard the lemon rind. Taste the sauce for seasoning and serve hot, sprinkled with the remaining chopped macadamia nuts, and sprigs of flat leaf parsley .

Serves 3–4
Preparation time: 15 minutes
Cooking time: about 20 minutes

Burmese Chicken Curry and Cellophane Noodles

This traditional Burmese dish is served with noodles. It is the ideal dish for an informal dinner party, as with its accompaniments, it is a meal in itself.

- 4 tablespoons groundnut oil
- 625 g/1¼ lb skinless, boneless chicken breasts, cut into bite-sized pieces
- 1½ teaspoons chilli powder
- ½ teaspoon turmeric
- ½ teaspoon salt
- 600 ml/1 pint coconut milk (see page 7)
- 300 ml/½ pint chicken stock
- 50 g/2 oz creamed coconut, chopped
- 375 g/12 oz cellophane noodles
- sesame oil
- salt

SPICE PASTE:

- 4 large garlic cloves, chopped
- 2 onions, chopped
- 1 large fresh red chilli, deseeded and chopped
- 2.5 cm/1 inch piece of fresh root ginger, chopped
- 1 teaspoon shrimp paste

ACCOMPANIMENTS:

- 3 spring onions, sliced
- 2 tablespoons crisply fried onion flakes (see page 9)
- 3 garlic cloves, sliced and crisply fried
- 2 tablespoons fresh coriander leaves
- 1 lemon, cut into wedges
- whole dried chillies, fried (optional)

1 First make the spice paste. Place the garlic, onions, chilli, ginger and shrimp paste in a food processor or blender and work to a thick paste.

2 Heat the groundnut oil in a large heavy-based saucepan, add the spice paste and fry over gentle heat, stirring constantly, for 5 minutes until softened.

3 Add the chicken pieces to the pan and fry, stirring constantly, for a further 5 minutes to seal. Stir in the chilli powder, turmeric, salt, coconut milk and stock. Bring the curry to the boil, then reduce the heat and simmer very gently, stirring occasionally, for 30 minutes or until the chicken pieces are tender.

4 Stir the creamed coconut into the curry and then simmer over medium heat for 2–3 minutes, stirring the mixture constantly, until the creamed coconut has dissolved and thickened the sauce slightly. Taste and adjust the seasoning if necessary.

5 Drop the noodles into a pan of salted boiling water. Bring the water back to the boil and cook the noodles for 3 minutes. Drain the noodles and stir through a little sesame oil.

6 To serve, divide the noodles among 4 deep soup bowls and ladle some chicken curry over each portion. Serve the accompaniments separately. The fried dried chillies should be nibbled with caution: they are extremely hot!

Serves 4

Preparation time: 15 minutes

Cooking time: 50 minutes

Chicken Korma with Green Beans

This is the perfect curry for those who find chillies too much for them. Korma curry powder is very mild, with little or no chilli, but including coriander, cumin, mustard seeds, fenugreek and bay leaves.

- **2 tablespoons vegetable oil**
- **375 g/12 oz skinless, boneless chicken breasts, cut into bite-sized pieces**
- **1 onion, sliced**
- **2½ tablespoons korma curry powder**
- **150 ml/¼ pint chicken stock**
- **1 teaspoon tomato purée**
- **2 teaspoons caster sugar**
- **75 g/3 oz tomatoes, roughly chopped**
- **150 ml/¼ pint single cream**
- **125 g/4 oz French beans, topped and tailed and cut into 2.5 cm/1 inch lengths**
- **25 g/1 oz ground almonds**
- **salt**
- **toasted flaked almonds, to garnish**

1 Heat the oil in a saucepan, add the chicken and onion, and fry over gentle heat, stirring occasionally, for 6 minutes or until the onion is soft and the chicken is lightly coloured. Stir in the curry powder and cook for a further 2 minutes.

2 Add the stock, tomato purée, sugar, tomatoes, cream and a little salt. Stir to combine the ingredients, bring to the boil, then reduce the heat, cover the pan and simmer gently for 10 minutes, stirring occasionally.

3 Stir the beans into the curry and cook, covered, for a further 15–20 minutes, stirring occasionally, until the chicken is cooked and the beans are tender. Stir the ground almonds into the curry and simmer for 1 minute to thicken the sauce. Taste and adjust the seasoning if necessary. Serve the korma hot, garnished with toasted flaked almonds.

Serves 4

Preparation time: 10–15 minutes

Cooking time: 40 minutes

Chicken Matsaman Curry

Matsaman is a corruption of the word Moslem and reflects the northern Indian influence on this curry from Thailand.

- 3 tablespoons vegetable oil
- 4 chicken drumsticks
- 350 ml/12 fl oz coconut milk (see page 7)
- 1½ tablespoons matsaman curry paste
- 3 new potatoes, scrubbed or peeled
- 1 onion, quartered
- ½ teaspoon lemon juice
- 1½ tablespoons Thai fish sauce (nam pla)
- ½ tablespoon sugar
- 25 g/1 oz roasted peanuts

1 Heat the oil in a large saucepan. Add the chicken drumsticks and brown on all sides. Stir the coconut milk into the pan and bring it to the boil. Add the curry paste. Lower the heat and simmer for 2 hours.

2 Stir in the potatoes, onion, lemon juice, fish sauce, sugar and peanuts, cover the pan and simmer for 20 minutes. Serve immediately.

Serves 4

Preparation time: 15 minutes

Cooking time: about 2½ hours

VARIATION

Beef Matsaman Curry

Replace the chicken with 750 g/1½ lb cubed stewing steak and proceed as in the main recipe.

Thai Green Chicken Curry

- 2 tablespoons groundnut oil
- 2.5 cm/1 inch piece of fresh root ginger, finely chopped
- 2 shallots, chopped
- 4 tablespoons Thai green curry paste (see page 8)
- 625 g/1¼ lb skinless, boneless chicken thighs, cut into 5 cm/2 inch pieces
- 300 ml/½ pint coconut milk (see page 7)
- 4 teaspoons Thai fish sauce (nam pla)
- 1 teaspoon palm sugar or soft brown sugar
- 3 kaffir lime leaves, shredded
- 1 green chilli, deseeded and sliced
- Thai basil leaves, to garnish (optional)

1 Heat the oil in a wok, add the ginger and shallots and fry over a gentle heat, stirring, for about 3 minutes or until softened. Add the green curry paste and fry for a further 2 minutes.

2 Add the chicken to the wok, stir to coat evenly in the spice mixture and fry for 3 minutes to seal the chicken. Stir the coconut milk into the curry, bring it to the boil, then reduce the heat and cook the curry gently, stirring occasionally, for 10 minutes or until the chicken is cooked through and the sauce has thickened.

3 Stir in the fish sauce, sugar, lime leaves and green chilli and cook the curry for a further 5 minutes. Taste and adjust the seasoning, if necessary, and serve the curry immediately, garnished with Thai basil leaves, if liked.

Serves 4

Preparation time: 10 minutes

Cooking time: 25 minutes

Chicken with Cashews

- 4 boneless, skinless chicken breasts, each weighing about 150 g/5 oz
- 2 tablespoons vegetable oil
- 1 bunch spring onions, sliced thinly on the diagonal
- 2 garlic cloves, crushed
- 125 g/4 oz cashews
- pepper

SAUCE:

- 2 teaspoons cornflour
- 6 tablespoons cold chicken stock or water
- 3 tablespoons soy sauce
- 2 tablespoons rice wine or dry sherry
- 2 teaspoons dark soft brown sugar

1 First prepare the sauce. Place the cornflour in a bowl, add 1 tablespoon of the stock or water and work to a paste. Stir in the remaining stock or water, the soy sauce, rice wine or sherry and sugar. Set aside.

2 Cut the chicken breasts into thin strips across the grain. Heat a wok until hot. Add the oil and heat over moderate heat until hot. Add the chicken strips, increase the heat to high and stir-fry for 3–4 minutes or until lightly coloured on all sides, then add the spring onions and garlic. Stir-fry for 1 further minute.

3 Stir the sauce to mix, then pour into the wok. Bring to the boil, stirring constantly. Add the cashews and toss to combine with the chicken and spring onions. Add pepper to taste and serve at once with rice.

Serves 3–4

Preparation time: 10 minutes

Cooking time: 10–15 minutes

Balti Chicken Vindaloo

- 1½ teaspoons coriander seeds
- 1½ teaspoons cumin seeds
- ¼ teaspoon black onion seeds (kalonji)
- ¼ teaspoon fenugreek seeds
- ¼ teaspoon mustard seeds
- 2.5 cm/1 inch piece of cinnamon stick
- 3 cloves
- ¾ teaspoon peppercorns
- 2 tablespoons desiccated coconut
- 2 tablespoons unsalted peanuts
- 6 tablespoons vinegar
- 2 garlic cloves, crushed
- 1 teaspoon chopped fresh root ginger
- ½ teaspoon turmeric
- 1½ teaspoons chilli powder
- 2 teaspoons salt
- 1.5 kg/3 lb chicken, skinned and cut into pieces
- 3 tablespoons vegetable oil
- 12 curry leaves
- 1 teaspoon cumin seeds
- fried onion rings (see page 8), to garnish

1 Dry roast the coriander, cumin, black onion, fenugreek, mustard, cinnamon, cloves, peppercorns, coconut and peanuts, then grind them in a spice grinder. Transfer to a bowl, then mix in the vinegar, garlic, ginger, turmeric, chilli powder and salt. Spread the mixture over the chicken pieces, cover and leave to marinate overnight.

2 Heat the oil in a Balti pan or wok, then add the curry leaves and cumin seeds. Cook for about 10 seconds, then add the chicken and cook, turning once or twice, for 15 minutes. Cover and continue cooking for a further 15–20 minutes or until the chicken is tender, adding a little water from time to time to keep the chicken moist. Leave over a very low heat for a few minutes before serving, garnished with the fried onion rings.

Serves 4–6

Preparation time: 20 minutes, plus marinating

Cooking time: 30–40 minutes

Chicken with Coconut Milk

- about 3 tablespoons oil
- 4 boneless, skinless chicken breasts, cut into 3 or 4 pieces
- 6 cardamom pods
- 6 cloves
- 5 cm/2 inch piece of cinnamon stick
- 1 large onion, finely sliced
- 2 garlic cloves
- 3.5 cm/1½ inch piece of fresh root ginger, peeled and chopped
- 3 green chillies, seeded
- juice of 1 lemon
- 1 teaspoon turmeric
- 50 g/2 oz creamed coconut
- 150 ml/¼ pint hot water
- salt
- strips of red pepper, to garnish

1 Heat the oil in a heavy-based saucepan, add the chicken and fry quickly all over. Remove with a slotted spoon and set aside.
2 Add a little more oil to the pan if necessary, and fry the cardamom, cloves and cinnamon for 1 minute. Add the onion and sauté gently for about 5 minutes until softened.
3 Place the garlic, ginger, chillies and lemon juice in a food processor or blender and work to a smooth paste. Add to the pan with the turmeric and cook for 5 minutes.
4 Melt the coconut in the hot water and add to the pan with salt to taste. Simmer for 2 minutes, then add the chicken pieces and any juices. Simmer for 15–20 minutes, until tender.
5 Transfer to a warmed serving dish, garnish with red pepper strips and serve immediately.

Serves 4
Preparation time: 10 minutes
Cooking time: 35–40 minutes

Kashmiri Chicken

- 50 g/2 oz ghee or butter
- 3 large onions, finely sliced
- 10 peppercorns
- 10 cardamom pods
- 5 cm/2 inch piece cinnamon stick
- 5 cm/2 inch piece of fresh root ginger, peeled and chopped
- 2 garlic cloves, finely chopped
- 1 teaspoon chilli powder
- 2 teaspoons paprika
- 1.5 kg/3 lb chicken pieces, skinned
- 250 g/8 oz natural yogurt
- salt

TO GARNISH:

- lime wedges
- chopped parsley

1 Melt the ghee or butter in a wok. Add the onions, peppercorns, cardamoms and cinnamon and fry for about 8–10 minutes, stirring occasionally, until the onions are golden. Add the ginger, garlic, chilli powder, paprika and salt to taste and fry for 2 minutes, stirring occasionally.
2 Add the chicken pieces and fry until they are evenly browned. Gradually add the yogurt, stirring constantly. Cover and cook for about 30 minutes, or until the chicken is cooked. Serve hot, garnished with lime wedges and the parsley.

Serves 4–6
Preparation time: 10 minutes
Cooking time: about 40 minutes

Chicken Tikka Masala

- 4 boneless, skinless chicken breasts, cubed
- juice of 1 lemon
- 1½ teaspoons salt
- 2 teaspoons pepper
- 1 onion, quartered
- 2 garlic cloves
- 5 cm/2 inch piece of fresh root ginger, peeled
- 375 g/12 oz natural yogurt
- chopped parsley or fresh coriander, to garnish

MASALA:

- 75 g/3 oz ghee or butter
- 1 onion, thinly sliced
- 1 garlic clove, thinly sliced
- 1½ teaspoons turmeric
- 1½ teaspoons chilli powder
- 1 teaspoon ground cinnamon
- seeds of 20 cardamom pods
- 1 teaspoon ground coriander
- 2 teaspoons aniseed

1 Place the chicken in a bowl and sprinkle with lemon juice, salt and pepper, mix to coat the chicken thoroughly, then cover and set aside.
2 Place the onion, garlic and ginger in a food processor or blender and chop finely. Add the yogurt and strain in the lemon juice from the chicken. Purée until blended, then pour over the chicken. Cover and marinate in the refrigerator for 24 hours.
3 Thread the chicken cubes on to kebab skewers, reserving the marinade. Place under a preheated grill and grill as slowly as possible for about 6–8 minutes until just cooked through. It is important not to overcook the chicken. Remove the chicken from the skewers.
4 Meanwhile, to make the masala, melt the ghee or butter in a wok, add the onion and garlic and fry for 4–5 minutes until soft. Sprinkle on the turmeric, chilli powder and cinnamon, stir well and fry for 1 minute. Add the cardamom, coriander and aniseed and stir-fry for 2 minutes, then add the reserved yogurt marinade. Mix well and bring to the boil. Add the chicken and cook for 5 minutes. Garnish with the chopped parsley and serve at once. Shredded spring onions make a pleasant accompaniment.

Serves 4–6
Preparation time: 45 minutes, plus marinating
Cooking time: about 20 minutes

Chicken Dhansak

- 250 g/8 oz channa dhal
- 250 g/8 oz moong dhal
- 1.2 litres/2 pints water
- 175 g/6 oz ghee
- 2 large onions, peeled and sliced
- 4 garlic cloves, peeled and sliced
- 6 cloves
- 6 cardamom pods
- 1½ teaspoons ground ginger
- 2 teaspoons garam masala
- 2½ teaspoons salt
- 1 chicken, weighing 1.5 kg/3 lb, skinned, boned and cut into 8 pieces
- 500 g/1 lb frozen whole leaf spinach
- 4 large tomatoes, chopped
- fried onion rings (see page 8) to garnish

1 Wash the dhals, place them in a large saucepan and add the water. Bring to the boil and simmer, covered, for 15 minutes.

2 Meanwhile, melt the ghee in a heavy pan, add the onions and garlic and fry gently for about 5 minutes until soft. Add the cloves, cardamom pods, ginger, garam masala and salt and fry for a further 3 minutes, stirring constantly.

3 Add the chicken and fry until browned on all sides, then remove from the pan with a slotted spoon and drain on kitchen paper.

4 Add the spinach and tomatoes to the pan and fry gently for 10 minutes, stirring occasionally.

5 Mash the dhals in the cooking water, then stir into the spinach mixture. Return the chicken to the pan, cover with a tight-fitting lid and simmer for 45 minutes or until the chicken is tender. Serve hot, garnished with fried onion rings.

Serves 4

Preparation time: 15 minutes

Cooking time: 1 hour 10 minutes

Balinese Duck Curry

- 4 tablespoons vegetable oil
- 1.5 kg/3 lb oven-ready duck, cut into 4 portions
- 1 stalk of lemon grass, halved lengthways
- 4 kaffir lime leaves, bruised
- 1 teaspoon salt
- 300 ml/½ pint water
- 2 teaspoons soft brown sugar
- 2 green chillies, sliced, to garnish

SPICE PASTE:

- 8 shallots, chopped
- 4 garlic cloves, chopped
- 6 large green chillies, deseeded and chopped, extra to garnish
- 5 cm/2 inch piece of fresh root ginger, chopped
- 2.5 cm/1 inch piece of fresh galangal, chopped
- 2 teaspoons turmeric
- ¼ teaspoon pepper
- 6 candlenuts or macadamia nuts (optional)

1 First make the spice paste. Put the shallots, garlic, green chillies, ginger, galangal, tumeric, pepper and candlenuts or macadamia nuts, if using, into a food processor or blender and work to a thick paste. Heat the vegetable oil in a wide sauté pan, add the paste and fry over gentle heat, stirring constantly, for about 3 minutes or until softened and fragrant.

2 Add the duck portions, lemon grass, lime leaves and salt to the pan. Stir to coat the duck evenly in the spice mixture and fry for a further 4 minutes to seal the meat. Add the water, stir well and bring to the boil. Reduce the heat, cover the pan and cook gently, stirring from time to time, for 45 minutes, until the duck is tender.

3 Remove the lid from the pan, stir in the sugar and increase the heat to moderate. Cook, stirring frequently, for a further 30 minutes, until the duck is cooked and the sauce is thick.

4 Skim off any surplus fat from the surface of the curry. Taste and adjust the seasoning if necessary. Serve hot, garnished with sliced chillies.

Serves 4

Preparation time: 25 minutes

Cooking time: 1½ hours

Meat Dishes

Pork in Coconut Milk

A Nonya dish from Malaysia, blending two cuisines – the Chinese love of pork and the Malaysian use of coconut milk.

2 onions, peeled and quartered
8 dried red chillies
6 macadamia nuts
½ teaspoon terasi (dried shrimp paste)
2 tablespoons vegetable oil
750 g/1½ lb lean pork, cut into 2.5 cm/1 inch cubes
250 ml/8 fl oz water
1 teaspoon salt
250 ml/8 fl oz thick coconut milk (see page 7)
1 tablespoon sugar
2 tablespoons lime or lemon juice

TO GARNISH:

dried red chillies
slices of fresh coconut
sprigs of fresh coriander

1 Put the onions, chillies, macadamia nuts, terasi and 1 tablespoon water into a food processor or blender and grind to a paste.
2 Heat the oil in a large saucepan and gently fry the paste, stirring, for 3–4 minutes. Add the pork and cook, stirring, until it changes colour and is well coated with the paste.
3 Pour in the water and add the salt. Cover and simmer gently for about 30 minutes until the pork is just tender.
4 Add the coconut milk and simmer uncovered for 10–15 minutes, stirring from time to time. Stir in the sugar and lime juice.
5 To serve, spoon the curry into individual bowls and garnish with dried chilli strips, fresh coconut and coriander sprigs.

Serves 4–6
Preparation time: 30 minutes
Cooking time: about 45 minutes

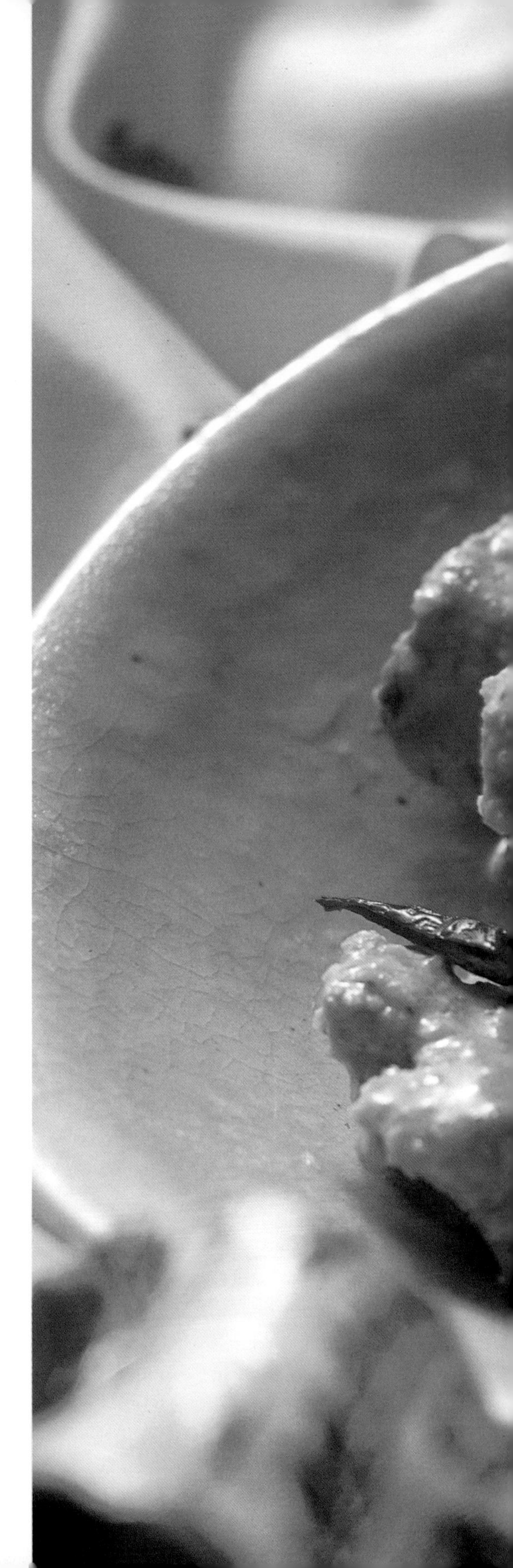

Raan

This is a dish for special occasions and, although it takes time to prepare with the lengthy marinating and slow roasting, it is quite simple to make. The two applications of spice paste give it a subtle depth of flavour.

- **2.5 kg/5 lb leg of lamb, skin and fat removed**
- **50 g/2 oz piece of fresh root ginger, peeled and chopped**
- **6 garlic cloves**
- **rind of 1 lemon**
- **juice of 2 lemons**
- **2 teaspoons cumin seeds**
- **6 cardamom pods, peeled**
- **1 teaspoon ground cloves**
- **1 teaspoon turmeric**
- **1½ teaspoons chilli powder**
- **1 tablespoon salt**
- **300 g/10 oz natural yogurt**
- **150 g/5 oz whole, unpeeled almonds**
- **4 tablespoons brown sugar**
- **1 teaspoon saffron threads, soaked in 3 tablespoons boiling water**

TO GARNISH:

- **mint leaves**
- **lime slices**

1 Prick the lamb all over with a fork and make about 12 deep cuts in the flesh. Place the ginger, garlic, lemon rind and juice, cumin seeds, cardamom pods, cloves, turmeric, chilli powder and salt in a food processor or blender and work to a paste. Spread the paste over the lamb and leave to stand, covered, for 1 hour in a flameproof casserole.

2 Blend 4 tablespoons of the yogurt with the almonds and 2 tablespoons of sugar. Stir in the remaining yogurt and pour over the lamb. Cover tightly and chill for 48 hours in the refrigerator.

3 Let the meat return to room temperature. Sprinkle with the rest of the sugar and cook, uncovered, in a preheated oven, 220°C (425°F), Gas Mark 7, for 30 minutes. Cover the casserole, lower the heat to 160°C (325°F), Gas Mark 3 and cook for 3 hours, basting occasionally. Sprinkle with the saffron water and cook for a further 30 minutes or until very tender.

4 Remove the meat from the casserole, wrap it in foil and keep warm. Skim off the fat from the casserole and boil the sauce until thick. Place the meat on a dish and pour over the sauce. Carve in thick slices to serve, and garnish with mint and lime slices.

Serves 6

Preparation time: 20 minutes, plus standing and marinating

Cooking time: about 4 hours

Oven temperature: 220°C (425°F), Gas Mark 7; then 160°C (325°F), Gas Mark 3

Lamb with Yogurt

- 4 tablespoons oil
- 3 onions, finely chopped
- 6 cardamom pods
- 5 cm/2 inch piece of cinnamon stick
- 1½ tablespoons ground coriander
- 2 teaspoons ground cumin
- ½ teaspoon turmeric
- ½ teaspoon ground cloves
- 1–2 teaspoons chilli powder
- ½ teaspoon grated nutmeg
- 1 tablespoon paprika
- 300 g/10 oz natural yogurt
- 750 g/1½ lb boned leg of lamb, cubed
- 1 large tomato, skinned and chopped
- salt
- sprigs of fennel, to garnish

1 Heat the oil in a large saucepan, add the onions, cardamom and cinnamon and fry for about 5 minutes.

2 Stir in the coriander, cumin, turmeric, cloves, chilli powder and nutmeg and fry until dry, then add 2 tablespoons water and cook, stirring, for 5 minutes, adding a little more water if necessary.

3 Add the paprika and slowly stir in the yogurt. Add the lamb, tomato and salt to taste and mix well. Bring to simmering point, cover and cook for 1 hour or until tender. Garnish with the fennel sprigs to serve.

Serves 4

Preparation time: 15 minutes

Cooking time: 1¼ hours

Roghan Ghosht

One of the best known of all curries from northern India.

- 4 tablespoons oil
- 2 onions, finely chopped
- 750 g/1½ lb boned leg of lamb, cubed
- 300 g/10 oz natural yogurt
- 2 garlic cloves
- 2.5 cm/1 inch piece of fresh root ginger, peeled and roughly chopped
- 2 green chillies, deseeded
- 1 tablespoon coriander seeds
- 1 teaspoon cumin seeds
- 1 teaspoon chopped mint leaves
- 1 teaspoon chopped fresh coriander
- 6 cardamom pods
- 6 cloves
- 2.5 cm/1 inch piece of cinnamon stick
- salt and pepper
- 125 g/4 oz flaked almonds

TO GARNISH:

- fried onion rings (see page 8)
- lemon slices

1 Heat 2 tablespoons of the oil in a large saucepan, add half of the onions and fry until golden.
2 Add the lamb and 175 g/6 oz of the yogurt, stir well, cover and simmer for 20 minutes.
3 Meanwhile, place the garlic, ginger, chillies, coriander seeds, cumin, mint, fresh coriander and 2–3 tablespoons of the yogurt in a food processor or blender and work to a paste.
4 Heat the remaining oil in a large saucepan, add the cardamom, cloves and cinnamon and fry for 1 minute, stirring. Add the remaining onion and the prepared spice paste and fry for 5 minutes, stirring constantly.
5 Add the lamb and yogurt mixture, season to taste, stir well and bring to simmering point. Cover and cook for 30 minutes.
6 Add the almonds and cook for a further 15 minutes, until the meat is tender. Garnish with fried onion rings and lemon slices and and serve immediately.

Serves 4
Preparation time: 20 minutes
Cooking time: about 1¼ hours

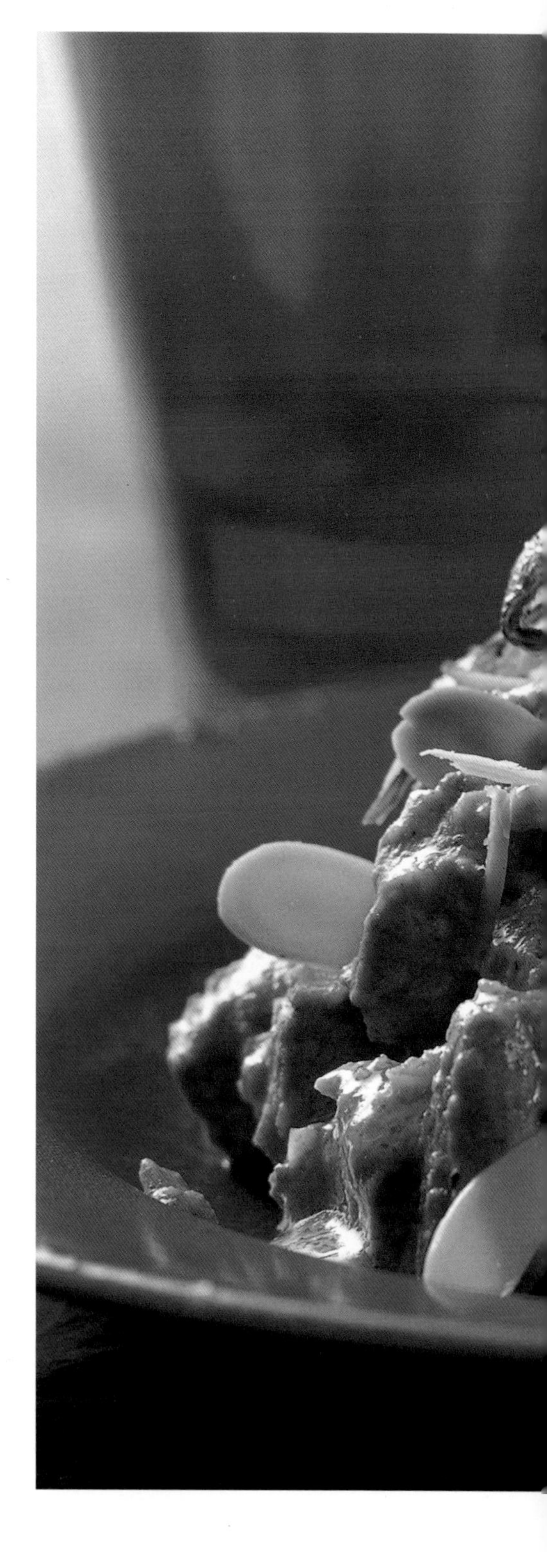

Kheema Dopiazah

Dopiazah describes a dish which contains double the normal quantity of onions. *Doh* means two or twice, and *piazah* means onions. The main feature of the *dopiazah* is that some of the onions are cooked with the meat, while the rest are added later to provide a contrast in texture.

- **500 g/1 lb onions**
- **4 tablespoons oil**
- **2.5 cm/1 inch piece of fresh root ginger, peeled and chopped**
- **1 garlic clove, finely chopped**
- **2 green chillies, finely chopped**
- **1 teaspoon turmeric**
- **1 teaspoon ground coriander seeds**
- **1 teaspoon ground cumin seeds**
- **750 g/1½ lb minced lamb**
- **150 g/5 oz natural yogurt**
- **1 x 225 g/7½ oz can tomatoes**
- **salt**
- **chopped fresh parsley, to garnish**

1 Finely chop 375 g/12 oz of the onions and thinly slice the remainder.
2 Heat 2 tablespoons of the oil in a large heavy-based saucepan, add the chopped onion and fry until golden. Add the ginger, garlic, chillies, turmeric, coriander and cumin and fry for 2 minutes. Add the lamb and cook, stirring, until well browned.
3 Stir in the yogurt, a spoonful at a time, until it is absorbed, then add the tomatoes with their juices, and salt to taste. Bring to the boil, stir well, then cover the pan and simmer for 20 minutes or until the meat is cooked.

4 Meanwhile, heat the remaining oil in a frying pan and fry the sliced onions until brown and crisp. To serve, transfer the meat mixture to a warmed serving dish and sprinkle with the fried onion and chopped parsley.

Serves 4
Preparation time: 20 minutes
Cooking time: about 50 minutes

Balti Kheema

- 2 tablespoons vegetable oil
- 500 g/1 lb green peppers, cored, deseeded and sliced
- 500 g/1 lb onions, sliced
- 2 teaspoons salt
- 2 teaspoons pepper
- ½ teaspoon ground cumin
- 2 teaspoons garam masala
- pinch of ground cinnamon
- 1½ teaspoons chilli powder
- 750 g/1½ lb minced lamb
- red onion rings, to garnish

1 Heat the oil in a Balti pan or heavy-based frying pan, add the peppers and stir-fry for about 1 minute. Remove the peppers with a slotted spoon and keep warm.

2 Add the onions to the oil and fry until they are golden brown. Add the salt, pepper, cumin, garam masala, cinnamon and chilli powder and stir-fry for 2 minutes.

3 Add the minced lamb and cook gently for about 20 minutes, stirring frequently to make sure that it does not stick to the bottom of the pan.

4 Return the green peppers to the pan and heat through over a low heat for a further 10 minutes. Garnish with onion rings and serve with poppadums.

Serves 4–6

Preparation time: 15 minutes

Cooking time: 35 minutes

Lamb Curry with Coconut

If fresh coconut is not available, blend the other spices and lemon juice as in step 1 and add 50 g/2 oz creamed coconut to the onions with the blended spices.

- 4 tablespoons oil
- 2 onions, chopped
- 4 curry leaves
- 750 g/1½ lb boned leg of lamb, cubed
- 1 x 225 g/ 7½ oz can tomatoes
- salt

SPICE PASTE:

- grated flesh of ½ fresh coconut
- 4 dried red chillies
- 1 teaspoon cumin seeds
- 1 tablespoon coriander seeds
- 1 tablespoon poppy seeds
- 1 teaspoon peppercorns
- 2.5 cm/1 inch piece of fresh root ginger, peeled and chopped
- 2 garlic cloves
- 1 teaspoon turmeric
- 2 tablespoons lemon juice

TO GARNISH:

- grated coconut
- 2 tablespoons finely chopped fresh coriander

1 First make the spice paste. Put the coconut, chillies, cumin, coriander and poppy seeds in a frying pan and dry-fry for about 1 minute. Place in a food processor or blender with the peppercorns, ginger, garlic, turmeric and lemon juice and blend to a paste.
2 Heat the oil in a large saucepan, add the onions and fry for about 5 minutes until softened, then add the curry leaves and the prepared spice paste and fry for 5 minutes.
3 Add the lamb and cook, stirring, for 5 minutes, then add the tomatoes with their juices and season with salt to taste. Bring to simmering point, cover and cook for about 1 hour, until tender.
4 To serve, sprinkle with grated coconut and chopped fresh coriander.

Serves 4
Preparation time: 20 minutes
Cooking time: about 1 hour 10 minutes

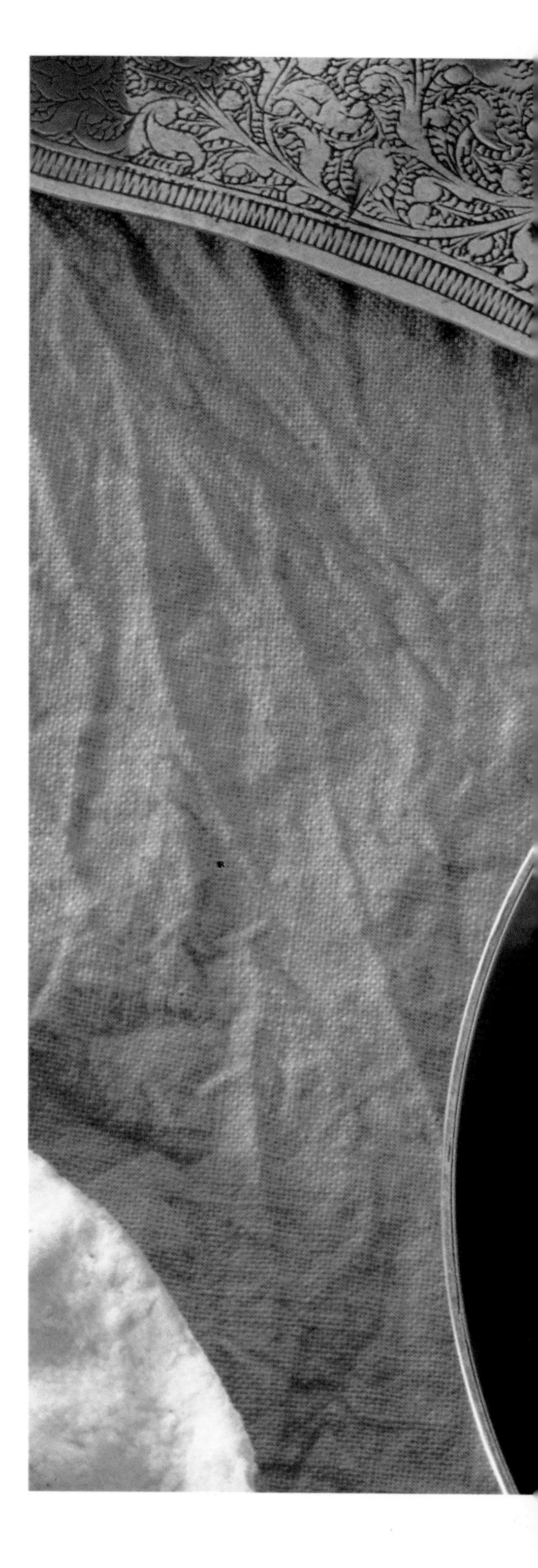

Stir-fried Lamb with Okra and Tomatoes

- 250 g/8 oz small okra, trimmed
- 3 tablespoons vegetable oil
- 1 onion, thinly sliced
- 1–2 garlic cloves, crushed
- 2 teaspoons ground coriander
- 2 teaspoons turmeric
- 1 teaspoon hot chilli powder, or to taste
- 500 g/1 lb lamb fillet, cut into thin strips across the grain
- 250 g/8 oz ripe tomatoes, skinned and chopped roughly
- finely grated rind and juice of ½ lemon
- ½ teaspoon caster sugar
- salt

1 Blanch the okra in boiling salted water for 5 minutes, then drain, rinse under cold running water and drain again. Set aside.

2 Heat a wok until hot. Add the oil and heat over moderate heat until hot. Add the onion, garlic, coriander, turmeric and chilli powder and stir-fry for 2–3 minutes or until the onion is softened, taking care not to let any of the ingredients brown.

3 Add the lamb strips, increase the heat to high and stir-fry for 3–4 minutes or until the lamb is browned on all sides.

4 Add the tomatoes and stir-fry until the juices run, then add the lemon rind and juice, sugar and salt to taste. Stir-fry to mix, then add the okra and toss for 3–4 minutes or until heated through. Serve hot with boiled rice.

Serves 4

Preparation time: 10 minutes

Cooking time: about 15 minutes

Thai Red Beef Curry

It is easy to produce an 'authentic' curry quickly, using either your own homemade Thai red curry paste, or one of the excellent ready-made versions now stocked by Asian shops and many supermarkets.

- **3 tablespoons groundnut oil**
- **3 tablespoons Thai red curry paste (see page 7)**
- **½ teaspoon ground coriander**
- **½ teaspoon ground cumin**
- **4 Kaffir lime leaves, shredded**
- **500 g/1 lb fillet of beef, cut into thin strips**
- **400 ml/14 fl oz coconut milk (see page 7)**
- **2 tablespoons crunchy peanut butter**
- **2 teaspoons Thai fish sauce (nam pla)**
- **1 tablespoon soft brown sugar**
- **sprigs of coriander, to garnish (optional)**

1 Heat the oil in a heavy-based saucepan and add the red curry paste, ground coriander and cumin and the lime leaves. Cook over gentle heat, stirring frequently, for 3 minutes.
2 Add the beef strips to the pan, stir to coat them evenly in the curry paste and cook gently, stirring frequently for 5 minutes.
3 Add half of the coconut milk to the pan, stir to combine and simmer gently for 4 minutes until most of the coconut milk has been absorbed.
4 Stir in the rest of the coconut milk with the peanut butter, fish sauce and sugar. Simmer gently for 5 minutes until the sauce is thick and the beef is tender. Garnish with coriander sprigs, if using, and serve immediately with steamed rice.

Serves 4
Preparation time: 5–10 minutes
Cooking time: about 20 minutes

Malaysian Beef and Potato Curry

- 2 tablespoons groundnut oil
- 5 shallots, chopped
- 2 garlic cloves, crushed
- 5 cm/2 inch piece of fresh root ginger, grated
- 2 tablespoons hot curry powder
- 1 teaspoon ground cinnamon
- 1 teaspoon ground cumin
- 1 teaspoon ground coriander
- ¼ teaspoon ground cardamom
- 4 curry leaves
- 1 star anise
- 4 cloves
- 375 g/12 oz sirloin steak, cut into 1 cm/½ inch strips
- 300 g/10 oz potatoes, peeled and cut into medium chunks
- 2 large red chillies, deseeded and finely chopped
- ½ teaspoon salt
- 300 ml/½ pint coconut milk (see page 7)
- juice of 1 lime
- 1 teaspoon soft brown sugar
- sliced red chillies, to garnish

1 Heat the oil in a saucepan, add the shallots, garlic and ginger, and fry over a gentle heat, stirring frequently, for 5 minutes or until softened.
2 Add the curry powder, cinnamon, cumin, coriander, cardamom, curry leaves, star anise and cloves, and fry for 1 minute.
3 Add the beef and stir well to coat it in the spice mixture. Add the potatoes, chillies, salt and coconut milk. Stir to combine, bring to the boil, then reduce the heat, cover the pan and simmer gently, stirring occasionally, for 40 minutes until the beef is tender and the potatoes are cooked.
4 Stir in the lime juice and sugar and cook uncovered for 2 minutes. Taste and adjust the seasoning, if necessary, and serve hot, garnished with sliced red chillies.

Serves 4
Preparation time: 20 minutes
Cooking time: 50 minutes

Simple Beef Curry with Spinach

If you would like to make this curry hotter, add some of the seeds from the green chillies to it.

- **2 tablespoons ghee or vegetable oil**
- **1 large onion, thinly sliced**
- **2 garlic cloves, crushed**
- **2 green chillies, deseeded and sliced**
- **2 cloves, bruised**
- **1 teaspoon garam masala**
- **1 teaspoon ground coriander**
- **1 teaspoon turmeric**
- **½ teaspoon chilli powder**
- **1½ teaspoons ground cumin**
- **625 g/1¼ lb fillet of beef, cut into bite-sized pieces**
- **1 teaspoon salt**
- **175 g/6 oz tomatoes, cut into large dice**
- **150 ml/¼ pint coconut milk (see page 7)**
- **250 g/8 oz ready-washed young leaf spinach**
- **1 teaspoon lemon juice**

1 Heat the ghee or oil in a saucepan, add the onion and garlic and fry over a gentle heat, stirring frequently, for about 5 minutes or until softened but not coloured. Stir in the chillies and fry for 2 minutes.
2 Add the cloves, garam masala, coriander, turmeric, chilli powder and cumin. Stir well to mix and fry, stirring constantly, for 2 minutes.
3 Stir in the beef and salt and cook, stirring, for 3 minutes to seal the meat, then add the diced tomatoes, coconut milk and spinach and stir to mix. Cover the pan and simmer gently, stirring very occasionally, for 20 minutes.
4 Stir in the lemon juice and cook the curry, uncovered, for a further 8–10 minutes, stirring occasionally, until the sauce has thickened. Taste and adjust the seasoning if necessary and serve immediately. Saffron rice would be a good accompaniment to this curry.

Serves 4
Preparation time: about 20 minutes
Cooking time: 35–40 minutes

Chilli Fry

This is a fairly dry curry, so take care not to let it stick to the pan.

- **4 tablespoons oil**
- **1 large onion, finely chopped**
- **½ teaspoon ground coriander seeds**
- **½ teaspoon turmeric**
- **2.5 cm/1 inch piece of fresh root ginger, finely chopped**
- **1 chilli, chopped**
- **500 g/1 lb frying steak, cut into 2.5 x 1 cm/ 1 x ½ inch strips**
- **1 green or red pepper, cored, deseeded and roughly chopped**
- **2 tomatoes, quartered**
- **juice of 1 lemon**
- **salt**

1 Heat the oil in a wok or frying pan, add the onion and fry for about 5 minutes until softened. Add the coriander, turmeric, ginger and chilli and fry over low heat for 5 minutes; if the mixture becomes dry, add 1 tablespoon water.

2 Add the steak, increase the heat and cook, stirring, until browned all over. Add the chopped pepper, cover and simmer gently for 5–10 minutes, until the meat is tender. Add the tomatoes, lemon juice and salt to taste and cook, uncovered, for 2–3 minutes.

Serves 4

Preparation time: 10–15 minutes

Cooking time: 25–30 minutes

Nargis Kebab

This is an Indian version of the Scotch egg – and may be served with or without the sauce.

- **250 g/8 oz minced beef**
- **2 garlic cloves, crushed**
- **2.5 cm/1 inch piece of fresh root ginger, peeled and grated**
- **½ teaspoon ground coriander seeds**
- **½ teaspoon ground cumin seeds**
- **½–1 teaspoon chilli powder**
- **¼ teaspoon ground cloves**
- **1 tablespoon cornflour**
- **salt**
- **1 egg yolk**
- **4 small hard-boiled eggs**
- **oil, for shallow frying**

SAUCE:

- **4 tablespoons oil**
- **5 cm/2 inch piece of cinnamon stick**
- **6 cloves**
- **6 cardamom pods**
- **1 onion, finely chopped**
- **2 garlic cloves, crushed**
- **2.5 cm/1 inch piece of fresh root ginger, peeled and grated**
- **2 teaspoons ground coriander seeds**
- **1 teaspoon ground cumin seeds**
- **½–1 teaspoon chilli powder**
- **4 tablespoons natural yogurt**
- **1 x 400 g/13 oz can tomatoes**
- **2 tablespoons chopped fresh coriander**

1 To make the kebabs, mix together the beef, garlic, ginger, coriander seeds, cumin, chilli powder, cloves and cornflour and add salt to taste. Bind with the egg yolk and divide the mixture into 4 equal parts.

2 With well-floured hands, flatten each portion into a round, place a hard-boiled egg in the centre and work the meat around to cover. Roll each one into a ball.

3 Heat the oil in a pan and shallow fry the kebabs until they are brown all over. Lift out with a slotted spoon and drain on kitchen paper. Set aside while making the sauce.

4 To make the sauce, heat the oil in a saucepan, add the cinnamon, cloves and cardamom and fry for a few seconds. Add the onion, garlic and ginger and fry until golden brown. Add the coriander seeds, cumin and chilli powder and fry for 1 minute. Add the yogurt, a spoonful at a time, stirring until it is absorbed before adding the next spoonful.

5 Break up the tomatoes with a fork, add them to the pan with their juices and simmer for 1 minute. Add the kebabs to the sauce, season with salt to taste and cook, uncovered, for 25 minutes until the sauce is thick. Stir in the chopped coriander to serve.

Serves 4

Preparation time: 15–20 minutes
Cooking time: about 45 minutes

Thai Fried Red Curry with Pork and Beans

- **175 g/6 oz French or runner beans, cut into 2.5 cm/1 inch lengths**
- **2 tablespoons vegetable oil**
- **300 g/10 oz pork fillet, thinly sliced**
- **2 tablespoons Thai red curry paste (see page 7)**
- **1 tablespoon Thai fish sauce (nam pla)**
- **1 tablespoon demerara sugar**

1 Place the beans in a medium saucepan. Add water to cover and bring to the boil. Cook for 5 minutes, then drain thoroughly in a colander. Set aside.

2 Heat the oil in a wok, add the pork and stir-fry for 6–8 minutes or until the pork is cooked. Using a slotted spoon, transfer the pork to a plate and set aside.

3 Add the curry paste to the oil remaining in the pan. Stir-fry for 3 minutes, then return the pork to the pan together with the fish sauce, sugar and cooked beans. Stir-fry for 10 minutes. Serve hot with boiled rice.

Serves 4

Preparation time: 10 minutes

Cooking time: 25–30 minutes

Brinjal Cutlets

In India, croquettes and patties of various sorts are known as cutlets.

- 2 large aubergines
- 3 tablespoons oil
- 1 onion, finely chopped
- 1 garlic clove, finely chopped
- 2 green chillies, deseeded and finely chopped
- 1 teaspoon turmeric
- 500 g/1 lb minced beef
- 1 egg, lightly beaten
- 2–3 tablespoons fresh breadcrumbs
- salt
- chopped fresh coriander, to garnish

1 Place the aubergines in a pan of boiling water and cook for 15 minutes or until they are almost tender. Drain them thoroughly in a colander and leave to cool.
2 Heat the oil in a saucepan, add the onion and fry until golden. Add the garlic, chillies and turmeric and fry for 2 minutes. Add the minced beef and cook, stirring, until brown all over. Add salt to taste and cook gently for 20 minutes until the meat is tender.
3 Cut the aubergines in half lengthways. Carefully scoop out the pulp, add it to the meat mixture and mix well. Taste and adjust the seasoning.
4 Using a spoon, carefully fill the aubergine shells with the mixture, brush with the egg and cover with breadcrumbs. Place the aubergines on a grill rack and cook under a preheated moderate grill for 4–5 minutes, until golden. Garnish with the chopped fresh coriander and serve at once with chilli sauce, if you like.

Serves 4
Preparation time: 10 minutes, plus cooling
Cooking time: 45 minutes

Burmese Pork Curry

- 2 tablespoons ghee
- 2 small onions, each cut into 8 wedges
- 4 garlic cloves, finely chopped
- 5 cm/2 inch piece of fresh root ginger, finely chopped
- 500 g/1 lb pork tenderloin, cut into 2.5 cm/1 inch cubes
- 1 teaspoon turmeric
- ½ teaspoon soft brown sugar
- 1 tablespoon mild curry paste
- 4 dried chillies, soaked in cold water for 10 minutes, then drained and finely chopped
- 2 stalks of lemon grass, quartered lengthways
- 1 teaspoon shrimp paste
- 150 ml/¼ pint vegetable stock
- 2 teaspoons soy sauce
- 2 fresh red chillies, thinly sliced, to garnish

1 Heat the ghee in a heavy-based saucepan, add the onion, garlic, ginger and pork and fry over a brisk heat, stirring constantly, for 4 minutes until lightly golden.

2 Lower the heat, stir in the turmeric, sugar, curry paste, dried chillies, lemon grass and shrimp paste and fry for 2 minutes.

3 Add the stock and soy sauce to the pan, stir to mix well, then bring the curry to the boil. Cover the pan, reduce the heat and cook the curry gently for 30 minutes, stirring occasionally, until the pork is tender. Discard the stalks of lemon grass. Taste, and adjust the seasoning if necessary. Serve the curry hot on a bed of flat rice noodles and garnish with the sliced red chillies.

Serves 4

Preparation time: 10 minutes

Cooking time: 45 minutes

Pork with Tamarind

- 50 g/2 oz dried tamarind
- 75 g/3 oz ghee or butter
- 2 large onions, sliced
- 8 garlic cloves, sliced
- 750 g/1½ lb lean pork, cubed
- ½ teaspoon paprika
- ½ teaspoon turmeric
- 1 teaspoon fenugreek seeds
- 25 g/1 oz fresh root ginger, peeled and chopped
- 2 fresh green chillies
- 1 teaspoon salt
- 1½ teaspoons garam masala
- 2 bay leaves
- 6 cardamom pods
- 3 cloves
- sprigs of coriander, to garnish

1 Put the tamarind into a bowl and pour over 300 ml/½ pint boiling water. Leave to soak for 30 minutes.
2 Melt the ghee or butter in a wok or heavy-based frying pan, add the onions and garlic and fry for 5 minutes until soft, then add the pork and stir-fry to seal the meat on all sides.
3 Add the paprika, turmeric, fenugreek, ginger, chillies and salt. Pour in 150 ml/¼ pint water, cover and cook for 20–30 minutes.
4 Mash the tamarind in the soaking water, then strain through a wire sieve set over a bowl, pressing the tamarind to extract as much pulp as possible.
5 Uncover the wok, bring to the boil and boil until nearly all the liquid has evaporated. Add the garam masala, bay leaves, cardamom pods, cloves and the tamarind pulp and cook over very low heat for about 30 minutes or until the pork is tender. Serve hot, garnished with the coriander sprigs.

Serves 4–6
Preparation time: 20 minutes, plus soaking
Cooking time: about 1¼ hours

Vegetable Dishes

Aubergines with Tomatoes

750 g/1½ lb aubergines, cut into 4 cm/1½ inch chunks
juice of 1 lemon
175 g/6 oz ghee or butter
2 onions, thinly sliced
4 garlic cloves, thinly sliced
7.5 cm/3 inch piece of fresh root ginger, peeled and thinly sliced
2 teaspoons black onion seeds (kalonji)
7.5 cm/3 inch piece cinnamon stick
2 teaspoons coriander seeds
2 teaspoons cumin seeds
2 teaspoons pepper
2 teaspoons salt
2 teaspoons garam masala
1½ teaspoons ground turmeric
1 teaspoon chilli powder
1 x 400 g/13 oz can chopped tomatoes
125 g/4 oz tomato purée
600 ml/1 pint boiling water
dried red chillies, to garnish

1 Place the aubergines in a bowl and stir in the lemon juice.
2 Melt the ghee or butter in a large wok, add the onions, garlic and ginger and fry gently for 4–5 minutes until soft. Add the black onion seeds, cinnamon, coriander and cumin seeds and stir well. Fry for a further 2 minutes, then stir in the pepper, salt, garam masala, turmeric and chilli powder.
3 Add the tomatoes with their juices and the tomato purée, stir well and bring to the boil. Pour in the boiling water and stir in the aubergine pieces with the lemon juice. Bring to the boil, lower the heat and simmer gently for 15–20 minutes until soft. Garnish with the dried red chillies and serve hot.

Serves 4–6
Preparation time: 15 minutes
Cooking time: 25–30 minutes

Spinach Paneer

Paneer is an Indian curd cheese available from all good Indian grocers.

- 250 g/8 oz paneer, cut into 2.5 cm/1 inch cubes
- 375 g/12 oz young leaf spinach, washed and dried
- 2 tablespoons ghee
- 1 large onion, chopped
- 2 garlic cloves, crushed
- 1 large green chilli, deseeded and sliced
- 1 tablespoon grated fresh root ginger
- 1 teaspoon turmeric
- 1 teaspoon ground coriander
- 1 teaspoon chilli powder
- ½ teaspoon ground cumin
- ½ teaspoon salt

1 Cut the paneer into 2.5 cm/1 inch cubes and set it aside. Steam the spinach for 3–4 minutes until it has wilted, leave it to cool and then place it in a food processor and blend briefly to a purée. Set aside.

2 Heat the ghee in a heavy-based saucepan, add the paneer cubes and fry, turning occasionally, for 10 minutes or until they are golden all over. Remove them from the pan with a slotted spoon and set aside.

3 Add the onion, garlic, chilli and ginger to the hot ghee and fry gently over low heat, stirring constantly, for 5 minutes until softened. Stir in the turmeric, ground coriander, chilli powder and cumin, and fry for 1 further minute.

4 Add the puréed spinach and the salt, stir well to combine, cover the pan and simmer gently for 5 minutes.

5 Stir in the fried paneer and cook, covered, for a further 5 minutes. Taste and adjust the seasoning if necessary, and serve immediately.

Serves 4

Preparation time: 15 minutes

Cooking time: 30 minutes

Kidney Bean Curry

- **125 ml/4 fl oz vegetable oil**
- **2 teaspoons cumin seeds**
- **1 large onion, chopped**
- **1 x 400 g/13 oz can chopped tomatoes**
- **1 tablespoon ground coriander**
- **1 teaspoon chilli powder**
- **1 teaspoon sugar**
- **1 teaspoon salt**
- **2 x 475 g/15 oz cans red kidney beans, drained**

1 Heat the oil in a wok or frying pan, add the cumin seeds and chopped onion and fry until the onion is lightly browned. Stir in the tomatoes and fry for a few seconds, then add the ground coriander, chilli powder, sugar and salt and stir well. Lower the heat and cook for about 5–7 minutes. Add the drained kidney beans, stir carefully but thoroughly and cook for 10–15 minutes. Serve immediately with rice.

Serves 4–6
Preparation time: 15 minutes
Cooking time: 30–35 minutes

Vegetables in Malaysian Coconut Sauce

This is a light and simple dish – and you can vary the vegetables according to what is available in the shops or in your garden.

- **125 g/4 oz broccoli florets**
- **125 g/4 oz French beans, cut into 2.5 cm/ 1 inch lengths**
- **1 red pepper, cored, deseeded and sliced**
- **125 g/4 oz courgettes, thinly sliced**

MALAYSIAN COCONUT SAUCE:

- **25 g/1 oz dried tamarind**
- **150 ml/¼ pint boiling water**
- **1 x 425 g/14 oz can thick coconut milk**
- **2 teaspoons Thai green curry paste (see page 8)**
- **1 teaspoon grated ginger**
- **1 onion, diced**
- **½ teaspoon turmeric**
- **salt**

1 First make the Malaysian coconut sauce. Put the tamarind into a bowl. Pour over the boiling water and leave to soak for 30 minutes.
2 Mash the tamarind in the soaking water, then strain through a wire sieve set over a bowl, pressing the tamarind to extract as much pulp as possible.
3 Skim 2 tablespoons of the cream from the coconut milk and place it in a wok or heavy-based saucepan. Add the curry paste, ginger, onion and turmeric and cook over gentle heat, stirring for 2–3 minutes. Stir in the remaining coconut milk and the tamarind water. Bring to the boil, then lower the heat and season with salt.
4 Add the broccoli and cook for 5 minutes, then add the French beans and red pepper and cook, stirring, for a further 5 minutes. Finally, stir in the courgettes and cook for 1–2 minutes. Prawn crackers make a nice accompaniment.

Serves 4
Preparation time: 15 minutes, plus standing
Cooking time: about 20 minutes

Masoor Dhal

- 4 tablespoons oil
- 3 cloves
- 2 teaspoons ground coriander
- 1 teaspoon turmeric
- 6 cardamom pods
- 2.5 cm/1 inch piece of cinnamon stick
- 1 onion, chopped
- 2.5 cm/1 inch piece of fresh root ginger, chopped
- 1 green chilli, finely chopped
- 1 garlic clove, chopped
- ½ teaspoon garam masala
- 250 g/8 oz masoor dhal (red split lentils)
- salt
- juice of 1 lemon
- sprigs of marjoram, to garnish

1 Heat the oil in a pan, add the cloves, ground coriander, turmeric, cardamom pods and cinnamon and fry until they start to swell. Add the onion and fry for about 5 minutes until translucent.
2 Add the ginger, chilli, garlic and garam masala and cook for 5 minutes.
3 Add the lentils, stir thoroughly and fry for 1 minute. Season to taste with salt and add enough water to come about 3 cm/1¼ inches above the level of the lentils. Bring to the boil, cover the pan and simmer for about 20 minutes, until the dhal is really thick and the lentils are tender.
4 Sprinkle with the lemon juice and stir to mix. Garnish with marjoram and serve immediately.

Serves 4
Preparation time: 15 minutes
Cooking time: about 35 minutes

Sweet Potato and Spinach Curry

- 500 g/1 lb sweet potato, peeled and cut into large chunks
- 3 tablespoons groundnut oil
- 1 red onion, chopped
- 2 garlic cloves, crushed
- 1 teaspoon shrimp paste
- 1 teaspoon turmeric
- 1 large fresh red chilli, deseeded and chopped
- 400 ml/14 fl oz coconut milk (see page 7)
- 250 g/8 oz ready-washed young leaf spinach
- salt

1 Cook the sweet potato chunks in a pan of salted boiling water for 8–10 minutes or until tender. Drain and set on one side.

2 Heat the oil in a saucepan, add the onion, garlic, shrimp paste and turmeric and fry over a gentle heat, stirring frequently, for 3 minutes. Stir in the chopped red chilli and fry for a further 2 minutes.

3 Add the coconut milk, stir to mix, and simmer for 3–4 minutes until the coconut milk has thickened slightly. Stir in the sweet potatoes, add salt to taste, and cook for 4 minutes.

4 Stir in the spinach, cover the pan and simmer gently for 2–3 minutes or until the spinach has wilted and the curry has heated through. Taste and adjust the seasoning if necessary and serve at once with naan or chapati.

Serves 4

Preparation time: about 10 minutes
Cooking time: about 25 minutes

New Potato Curry

- 5 cm/2 inch piece of fresh root ginger, peeled and grated
- 2 garlic cloves, crushed
- 50 g/2 oz ghee or butter
- 2 large onions, finely chopped
- 2 bay leaves
- 1 cinnamon stick, broken into short lengths
- 2 teaspoons fennel seeds
- 3 green cardamom pods
- 1 teaspoon turmeric
- 1 kg/2 lb small new potatoes, scrubbed
- 600 ml/1 pint water
- 300 ml/½ pint natural yogurt
- salt and pepper

TO GARNISH:

- chilli powder (optional)
- sprigs of coriander

1 Mix together the grated ginger and crushed garlic in a small bowl.

2 Place the ghee or butter in a large saucepan or wok and heat. Add the chopped onions, the ginger mixture, bay leaves, broken cinnamon stick, fennel seeds, cardamoms and turmeric to the melted fat. Fry the mixture gently, stirring constantly, until the onion is soft but not browned.

3 Add the potatoes to the pan, pour in the water and season to taste. Bring to the boil then cover the pan.

4 Simmer the curry steadily for 10 minutes, then uncover the pan and cook fairly rapidly for a further 10 minutes or until most of the water has evaporated.

5 Pour the natural yogurt over the potatoes and heat through fairly gently, to avoid curdling the sauce.

6 Transfer the curry to a serving dish and sprinkle with chilli powder to taste, if using, and coriander sprigs before serving.

Serves 4

Preparation time: 10 minutes

Cooking time: 30–35 minutes

Cauliflower Pachadi

This is a traditional dish from Kerala in southern India, in which cauliflower is marinated in buttermilk before cooking.

- **375 g/12 oz cauliflower florets**
- **150 ml/¼ pint buttermilk**
- **1 teaspoon salt**
- **3 tablespoons ghee**
- **1 large onion, thinly sliced**
- **2 garlic cloves, crushed**
- **1 tablespoon freshly grated root ginger**
- **1 teaspoon yellow mustard seeds**
- **1 teaspoon black mustard seeds**
- **1 teaspoon turmeric**
- **25 g/1 oz desiccated coconut**
- **150 ml/¼ pint water**
- **2 tablespoons chopped fresh coriander**
- **pepper**

1 Place the cauliflower florets in a bowl with the buttermilk, salt and some pepper. Mix well to combine the ingredients then cover and set aside for 2 hours to allow the cauliflower to marinate.

2 Heat the ghee in a heavy-based saucepan, add the onion, garlic and ginger and fry over gentle heat, stirring occasionally, for about 8 minutes until softened and lightly golden.

3 Add the 2 types of mustard seeds, the turmeric and coconut and cook for 3 minutes, stirring constantly.

4 Stir in the cauliflower with its buttermilk marinade and the water. Bring the curry to the boil, then reduce the heat, cover the pan and simmer gently for 12 minutes or until the cauliflower is tender.

5 Remove the lid, taste and adjust the seasoning if necessary and stir in the chopped coriander. Increase the heat and cook for a further 3–4 minutes to thicken the sauce. Serve hot as an accompaniment to other curries, with steamed rice or naan bread.

Serves 4

Preparation time: about 10 minutes, plus marinating

Cooking time: about 30 minutes

Aloo Gobi

Potatoes and cauliflower are both available in India, although they tend to be found only in the more temperate regions. Aloo Gobi is a good example of the way in which Indian cuisine has adapted itself to vegetables which have been introduced from other countries.

- **175 g/6 oz ghee**
- **1 kg/2 lb potatoes, peeled and chopped into 2.5 cm/1 inch pieces**
- **2 large onions, peeled and sliced**
- **4 garlic cloves, peeled and sliced**
- **2 teaspoons chilli powder**
- **1 teaspoon ground turmeric**
- **1 teaspoon ground coriander**
- **2 teaspoons salt**
- **½ teaspoon pepper**
- **1.2 litres/2 pints water**
- **500 g/1 lb cauliflower florets**
- **2 teaspoons garam masala**
- **lime slices, to garnish (optional)**

1 Melt the ghee in a large heavy-based pan, add the potatoes and fry gently for exactly 1 minute. Remove from the pan with a slotted spoon and set aside.
2 Add the onions and garlic to the pan and fry gently for about 5 minutes until soft. Add the chilli powder, turmeric, ground coriander, salt and pepper and fry for a further 3 minutes, stirring constantly.
3 Return the potatoes to the pan, add the water and bring to the boil. Lower the heat and simmer for 10 minutes.
4 Add the cauliflower and simmer for 15 minutes until the vegetables are tender and the sauce is thick.
5 Increase the heat to boil off any excess liquid if necessary. Stir in the garam masala, garnish with lime slices, if using, and serve hot.

Serves 4
Preparation time: 10 minutes
Cooking time: 30 minutes

Hot-tossed Cauliflower with Almonds

This recipe can be used for broccoli as well as cauliflower, with equally good results, and the almonds can be replaced with cashews or pine kernels, if you prefer.

- **1 medium cauliflower**
- **50 g/2 oz blanched almonds**
- **2 tablespoons vegetable oil**
- **1 onion, finely chopped**
- **2.5 cm/1 inch piece of fresh root ginger, peeled and finely chopped**
- **2 garlic cloves, crushed**
- **2 teaspoons ground coriander**
- **1 teaspoon turmeric**
- **½ teaspoon chilli powder**
- **75 ml/3 fl oz water**
- **salt**

1 Break the leaves off the cauliflower and reserve some of the small green leaves. Separate the florets from the stalks. Break the florets into individual sprigs and slice the stalks thinly on the diagonal. Blanch the stalks and sprigs in boiling salted water for 2 minutes. Drain, rinse immediately under cold running water and drain again.
2 Heat a wok until hot. Add the almonds and dry-fry over a gentle heat until toasted on all sides. Remove the wok from the heat and tip the toasted almonds on to a chopping board. Chop the almonds coarsely.
3 Return the wok to moderate heat. Add the oil and heat until hot. Add the onion, ginger, garlic, ground coriander, turmeric and chilli powder and stir-fry for 2–3 minutes or until softened, taking care not to let any of the ingredients brown.
4 Add the cauliflower sprigs and stalks and sprinkle over the water and add salt to taste. Increase the heat to high and stir-fry for 2–3 minutes or until the cauliflower is tender but still crisp.
5 Taste and add more salt if necessary. Serve at once, sprinkled with the chopped toasted almonds and garnished with the reserved green cauliflower leaves.

Serves 4
Preparation time: 10 minutes
Cooking time: 10 minutes

Balti Courgettes

- 25 g/1 oz ghee or butter
- 1 small onion, chopped
- pinch of asafoetida (optional)
- 2 small potatoes, quartered
- 375 g/12 oz courgettes, sliced
- ½ teaspoon chilli powder
- ½ teaspoon ground turmeric
- 1 teaspoon ground coriander
- ½ teaspoon salt
- 150 ml/¼ pint water
- ½ teaspoon garam masala
- chopped fresh coriander, to garnish

1 Heat the ghee or butter in a Balti pan or heavy-based frying pan, add the onion and fry for 5 minutes, stirring occasionally, until softened.

2 Add the asafoetida, if using, then add the potatoes and fry for about 2–3 minutes.

3 Stir in the sliced courgettes, the chilli powder, turmeric, coriander and salt. Add the water, cover the pan and cook gently for 8–10 minutes until the potatoes are tender. Sprinkle with the garam masala and garnish with chopped coriander leaves. Serve at once with an Indian bread.

Serves 4

Preparation time: 10 minutes

Cooking time: about 15 minutes

Braised Okra with Chillies

- 50 g/2 oz ghee or butter
- 1 large onion, sliced
- 3 garlic cloves, sliced
- 5 cm/2 inch piece fresh root ginger, peeled and finely chopped
- 2 fresh green chillies, deseeded and finely chopped
- ½ teaspoon chilli powder
- 500 g/1 lb okra, trimmed
- 200 ml/7 fl oz water
- 2 teaspoons desiccated coconut
- salt

1 Melt the ghee or butter in a large wok or heavy-based saucepan, add the onion, garlic, ginger, chillies and chilli powder and fry gently for 4–5 minutes until soft, stirring occasionally.
2 Add the okra, water and salt to taste. Bring to the boil, then lower the heat, cover and simmer for 5–10 minutes until the okra are just tender but still firm to the bite. Stir in the coconut and serve hot.

Serves 4
Preparation time: 15 minutes
Cooking time: about 15 minutes

Aubergine Petjal

The English translation for this Indonesian dish is Aubergine and Peanut Curry. It goes very well with the Indonesian Spiced Coconut Rice on page 82. Sambal oelek is a very hot sauce made from chillies and vinegar so use it sparingly.

- ½ teaspoon salt
- 750 g/1½ lb aubergines, cut into 2.5 cm/1 inch cubes
- 3 tablespoons groundnut oil
- 4 shallots, chopped
- 2 garlic cloves, crushed
- 1 teaspoon dried shrimp paste
- ½ teaspoon ground galangal (laos powder)
- 250 ml/8 fl oz coconut milk (see page 7)
- 1 teaspoon tamarind paste
- 1 tablespoon dark soy sauce
- 1 tablespoon sambal oelek
- 1 tablespoon palm sugar or soft brown sugar
- 125 g/4 oz roasted peanuts, coarsely ground

1 Rub the salt all over the aubergine cubes and place them in a steamer above a pan of boiling water. Steam for about 5 minutes until just tender. Drain and set aside.
2 Heat the oil in a wok, add the shallots and garlic, and fry over a gentle heat, stirring frequently, for about 5 minutes or until softened. Add the shrimp paste and galangal (laos) powder and fry for 3 minutes.
3 Add the coconut milk, tamarind paste, soy sauce, sambal oelek and sugar. Stir well and simmer gently for 3 minutes. Stir the steamed aubergine into the sauce and cook gently for a further 5 minutes. Add the ground peanuts to the curry and cook gently for 2 minutes.
4 Serve immediately with rice.

Serves 6
Preparation time: about 10 minutes
Cooking time: 25 minutes

Rice, Breads, Side Dishes and Chutneys

Indonesian Spiced Coconut Rice

375 g/12 oz basmati rice
125 g/4 oz creamed coconut, chopped
7 cm/3 inch piece of lemon grass, halved lengthways
5 cm/2 inch piece of cinnamon stick, broken in half
4 curry leaves
½ teaspoon ground nutmeg
¼ teaspoon ground cloves
1 teaspoon salt
pinch of pepper

1 Place the rice in a sieve and wash it thoroughly under cold water. Drain and place in a large heavy-based saucepan. Dissolve the creamed coconut in 750 ml/1¼ pints boiling water. Add the coconut milk to the rice with the lemon grass, cinnamon, curry leaves, nutmeg, cloves and salt and pepper.
2 Bring the rice to the boil and then boil, uncovered, over moderate heat for 8 minutes, stirring frequently, until almost all the liquid is absorbed.
3 Reduce the heat to low, cover the pan with a tightly fitting lid and cook the rice very gently for a further 10 minutes.
4 Remove the pan from the heat and, working quickly, loosen the rice grains with a fork. Cover the pan with a clean, dry tea towel and allow the rice to cook in its own heat for a further 15 minutes. Serve immediately.

Serves 6
Preparation time: 5 minutes
Cooking time: 35 minutes

Chapati

- 250 g/8 oz wholemeal flour
- 1 teaspoon salt
- about 200 ml/⅓ pint water
- ghee or oil, for frying

1 Place the flour and salt in a bowl. Make a well in the centre, then gradually stir in the water and work to a soft, supple dough. Knead for 10 minutes, then cover and leave in a cool place for 30 minutes.
2 Knead again very thoroughly, then divide the dough into 12 pieces. Roll out each piece on a floured surface into a thin round pancake.
3 Lightly grease a griddle or heavy-based frying pan with a little ghee or oil and place over moderate heat. Add a chapati and cook until blisters appear. Press down with a fish slice, then turn and cook the other side until lightly coloured. Remove from the pan and keep warm while cooking the rest.
4 Brush a little butter on one side and serve warm as soon as possible.

Makes 12
Preparation time: 30 minutes, plus standing
Cooking time: 12 minutes

Paratha

Parathas are essentially fried chapatis. They are very filling, so only allow about 1½ per person. They are shown on the left of the picture.

- 250 g/8 oz wholemeal flour
- 1 teaspoon salt
- about 200 ml/⅓ pint water
- 50–75 g/2–3 oz melted ghee or butter

1 Make the dough as for Chapati (see left) and divide into 6 pieces. Roll out each piece on a floured surface into a thin circle. Brush with melted ghee or butter and fold in half; brush again and fold in half again. Roll out again to a circle about 3 mm/⅛ inch thick.
2 Lightly grease a griddle or heavy-based frying pan with a little ghee or butter and place over moderate heat. Add a paratha and cook for 1 minute. Lightly brush the top with a little ghee or butter and turn over. Brush all round the edge with ghee or butter and cook until golden. Remove from the pan and keep warm while cooking the rest. Serve hot.

Makes 6
Preparation time: 30 minutes
Cooking time: 15 minutes

Puri

A traditional Indian breakfast often includes this deep-fried bread served with a selection of chutneys.

- **250 g/8 oz plain wholemeal flour**
- **½ teaspoon salt**
- **about 125–175 ml/4–6 fl oz water**
- **vegetable oil, for deep-frying**

1 Sift the flour and salt into a bowl and make a well in the centre. Gradually add just enough water to make a dough. Knead well for 5–10 minutes, cover with a damp tea towel and set aside for about 30 minutes.
2 Divide the dough into 12–14 pieces. Working on a lightly floured surface roll out each piece of dough into a flat 7 cm/ 3 inch round.
3 Heat the oil in a large saucepan to 180–190°C (350–375°F), or until a cube of bread browns in 30 seconds. Slide in one puri at a time and fry on both sides until golden brown. It will quickly swell up in the oil.
4 Lift out the puri with a slotted spoon, and drain on kitchen paper. Continue frying the puris and stack in layers, alternating the thin and thick sides to prevent them sticking. Keep wrapped in a clean tea towel or place in a covered container while you fry the remaining puris. Serve hot.

Makes 12–14
Preparation time: 20 minutes, plus standing
Cooking time: about 30 minutes

Naan

- 15 g/½ oz fresh yeast
- ¼ teaspoon sugar
- 2 tablespoons warm water
- 500 g/1 lb self-raising flour
- 1 teaspoon salt
- 150 ml/¼ pint tepid milk
- 150 ml/¼ pint natural yogurt (at room temperature)
- 2 tablespoons melted butter or cooking oil

TO GARNISH:

- 2–3 tablespoons melted butter
- 1 tablespoon poppy or sesame seeds

1 Put the yeast into a small bowl with the sugar and water. Mix well until the yeast has dissolved, then leave in a warm place for 15 minutes or until the mixture is frothy.
2 Sift the flour and salt into a large bowl. Make a well in the centre and pour in the yeast, milk, yogurt and butter or oil. Mix well to a smooth dough and turn on to a floured surface. Knead well for about 10 minutes, until smooth and elastic.
3 Place in a bowl, cover with clingfilm and leave to rise in a warm place for 1–1½ hours, or until doubled in size.
4 Turn the dough on to a floured surface, knead for a few minutes, then divide into 6 pieces. Pat or roll each piece into a round.
5 Place on a warmed baking sheet and bake in a preheated oven, 240°C (475°F), Gas Mark 9, for 10 minutes.
6 Brush the naans with butter and sprinkle with the poppy or sesame seeds. Serve warm.

Makes 6
Preparation time: about 45 minutes, plus standing and rising
Cooking time: 10 minutes
Oven temperature: 240°C (475°F), Gas Mark 9

Kachori

- 250 g/8 oz plain wholemeal flour
- ½ teaspoon salt
- about 125–175 ml/4–6 fl oz water

FILLING:

- 50 g/2 oz lentils, washed and soaked for 3 hours
- ½ teaspoon cumin seeds
- ½ teaspoon aniseed
- 1–2 tablespoons vegetable oil
- pinch of asafoetida (optional)
- 1 small fresh green chilli, deseeded and very finely chopped, or ½ teaspoon chilli powder
- pinch of salt
- vegetable oil, for deep-frying

TO GARNISH:

- onion slices
- lime rings
- coriander, chopped

1 Sift the flour and salt and make a well in the centre. Gradually add just enough water to make a dough. Knead well for 5–10 minutes, then cover with a damp tea towel and set aside.
2 To make the filling, drain the lentils and grind to a thick, coarse paste with a little water. Heat a wok or heavy-based frying pan, add the cumin seeds and aniseeds and dry-fry for 30 seconds then grind coarsely. Heat 1 tablespoon of oil in the wok and sprinkle in the asafoetida, if using, and the lentil paste. Add the chilli or chilli powder and salt. Fry for 5 minutes, adding a little more oil if necessary. Leave to cool.
3 Divide the dough into 12–14 pieces. Roll each piece into a ball and make a depression in the middle. Press about 1 teaspoon of filling into the depression and reshape the dough into a ball, encircling the filling. Carefully roll out into a 7 cm/3 inch round.
4 Heat 5–6 cm/2–2½ inches of oil in a large saucepan and fry the kachoris a few at a time until golden brown on both sides. Remove with a slotted spoon and drain on kitchen paper. Keep warm while frying the remaining kachoris. Serve hot with a chutney.

Makes 12–14
Preparation time: 30 minutes, plus soaking
Cooking time: about 30 minutes

Pilau Rice

- 3 tablespoons oil
- 5 cm/2 inch piece of cinnamon stick
- 4 cardamom pods
- 4 cloves
- 1 onion, sliced
- 250 g/8 oz basmati rice, washed and soaked for 30 minutes
- 600 ml/1 pint beef stock or water
- salt
- fried onion rings (see page 8), to serve (optional)

1 Heat the oil in a large heavy-based saucepan, add the cinnamon, cardamom and cloves and fry for a few seconds. Add the sliced onion and fry until golden.

2 Drain the rice thoroughly, add to the pan and fry, stirring occasionally, for 5 minutes.

3 Add the stock or water and season to taste with salt. Bring to the boil, then simmer, uncovered, for 10 minutes until the rice is tender and the liquid absorbed. To serve, garnish with fried onion rings, if liked.

Serves 4
Preparation time: 10 minutes, plus soaking
Cooking time: about 20 minutes

VARIATION

Vegetable Pilau

Add 125 g/4 oz each shelled peas, thinly sliced carrots and cauliflower florets to the pan after frying the onion. Fry for 5 minutes, then add the rice and proceed as in the main recipe.

Pineapple Chutney

Try this tangy chutney as an unusual alternative to classic mango chutney.

- **1 large, ripe pineapple, peeled, cored and chopped into small pieces**
- **3 shallots, chopped**
- **1 green chilli, deseeded and finely chopped**
- **1 tablespoon finely chopped fresh root ginger**
- **25 g/1 oz raisins**
- **125 g/4 oz soft brown sugar**
- **125 ml/4 fl oz distilled malt vinegar**
- **¼ teaspoon salt**

1 Place the pineapple in a heavy-based saucepan with the shallots, chilli, ginger, raisins, sugar, vinegar and salt. Cook over moderate heat, stirring constantly, until the sugar has dissolved. Bring the mixture to the boil, then reduce the heat a little and cook on a steady boil for 8–10 minutes, stirring occasionally, until most of the liquid has evaporated and the chutney is thick.

2 Pour the hot chutney into sterilized jars, seal, label and store. Once opened the chutney will keep well for 3–4 weeks in the refrigerator. Serve with poppadums or as an accompaniment to curries.

Makes about 475 g/15 oz chutney

Preparation time: 10 minutes

Cooking time: 15 minutes

Mango Chutney

The concentrated flavour of dried mangoes makes this a particularly fruity-tasting chutney. It can be stored in a cool place for up to 2–3 months.

- **250 g/8 oz dried mangoes, soaked in cold water overnight**
- **1 teaspoon chilli powder**
- **6 cardamom pods, bruised**
- **3 cloves**
- **1 teaspoon black mustard seeds**
- **1 teaspoon coriander seeds, lightly crushed**
- **5 black peppercorns, lightly crushed**
- **1 small cinnamon stick, broken in half**
- **375 g/12 oz fresh mango flesh, cut into 1 cm/1½ inch cubes**
- **1 large garlic clove, sliced thinly**
- **½ teaspoon salt**
- **300 ml/½ pint white wine vinegar**
- **375 g/12 oz caster sugar**

1 Drain the dried mangoes, reserving 300 ml/½ pint of the soaking liquid and cut into 1.5 cm/¾ inch pieces.
2 Place the chilli powder, cardamom pods, cloves, mustard seeds, coriander seeds, peppercorns and cinnamon stick in a large heavy-based saucepan. Dry-fry the spices over gentle heat, stirring frequently, for 2–3 minutes until fragrant.
3 Add the reserved mango soaking liquid, the chopped dried and the fresh mangoes, the garlic, salt and vinegar to the spices. Bring the mixture to the boil, then reduce the heat and simmer gently for 10 minutes, stirring occasionally.
4 Add the sugar and stir over a gentle heat until it has dissolved. Raise the heat and boil the chutney, stirring frequently, until it is thick. This will take about 40 minutes.
5 Ladle the chutney into sterilized jars, seal, label and store.

Makes about 1 kg/2 lb chutney
Preparation time: 20 minutes, plus overnight soaking
Cooking time: 55 minutes

Papaya and Coriander Raita

This cooling accompaniment can be made with fresh mango instead of the papaya.

- **175 g/6 oz natural yogurt**
- **½ ripe papaya, peeled, deseeded and diced**
- **2 tablespoons chopped fresh coriander**
- **½ teaspoon finely grated lime zest**
- **1 teaspoon lime juice (or more, according to taste)**
- **salt**

1 Place the yogurt, papaya, coriander, lime zest and juice in a bowl; season with salt and mix gently to combine. Taste and adjust the seasoning, adding more lime juice if liked.

2 Cover the raita and leave in the refrigerator for 30 minutes before serving to allow all the flavours to develop. Serve with curries or as a dip.

Serves 4

Preparation time: 10 minutes, plus chilling

Cucumber and Mint Raita

This refreshing raita goes particularly well with lamb dishes.

- **175 g/6 oz natural yogurt**
- **75 g/3 oz cucumber, cut into matchstick strips**
- **2 tablespoons chopped fresh mint**
- **pinch of ground cumin**
- **lemon juice, to taste**
- **salt**

1 Place the yogurt, cucumber and mint in a bowl. Add the cumin and lemon juice to taste and season with a little salt.
2 Cover the bowl and leave in the refrigerator for at least 30 minutes before serving to allow all the flavours to develop.

Serves 4
Preparation time: 10 minutes, plus chilling

VARIATION

Banana and Coconut Raita

For a cooling raita to serve with hot curries from southern India and other parts of the tropics, omit the cucumber, mint and cumin. Add 2 small thinly sliced bananas, 2 tablespoons toasted desiccated coconut and a pinch of chilli powder to the yogurt and stir gently to mix. Add lemon juice to taste and season with salt. Serve immediately.

Green Bean Sambal

This sambal makes a very good accompaniment to both Indonesian and Malaysian curries.

- 2 tablespoons vegetable oil
- 4 shallots, thinly sliced
- 2 garlic cloves, crushed
- ¼ teaspoon shrimp paste
- 250 g/8 oz French beans, topped, tailed and sliced thinly on an acute angle
- 2 teaspoons sambal oelek (hot pepper condiment)
- 1 teaspoon soft brown sugar
- salt

1 Heat the oil in a frying pan, add the shallots, garlic and shrimp paste and fry over a low heat, stirring frequently, for 5 minutes until the shallots are softened.
2 Add the beans, increase the heat to moderate and fry, stirring occasionally, for 8 minutes, until the beans are cooked but not too soft.
3 Stir in the sambal oelek, sugar and a little salt and continue frying the beans for 1 further minute. Taste and add a little more salt if necessary. Serve the sambal hot.

Serves 4
Preparation time: 15 minutes
Cooking time: 15 minutes

Recipe photographers:
Reed International Books Ltd./
Jeremy Hopley/Graham Kirk/
James Murphy/Alan Newnham/
Charlie Stebbings
Jacket Photographer:
Graham Kirk
Jacket Home Economist:
Sunil Vijayaker